dear joey,

dear joey,

*Embracing Everyday of Motherhood,
As If Your Last.*

Alicia Eggers

This book is dedicated to my Dad, who taught me how to dream. A dream we've shared for always. I love you.

Contents

prologue

On November 10, 2015, I wrote the blog post that inspired this book. I had no intention of even writing that mild November afternoon. I was exhausted. Severe chronic fatigue and anxiety halted my days. I had laid down with my three-year-old in my bedroom for a much needed time of rest. As is typical for me, I laid there and just let my thoughts run wild. This can be a blessing and a curse for me.

It wasn't long before God flooded my mind with the photo I encountered online the night before. The photo was of Joey and Indy in her hospital bed.

I took out my phone, opened my blogging app, and witnessed my thumbs dance rapidly across the screen. Ten minutes' total was all it took from title to tagging. I proof-read it twice, hit submit, and thought to myself "nobody is gonna read this anyway."

By early evening, I was curious to check my blog stats. This familiar ritual usually leaves me feeling a bit defeated, but hopeful. As a writer and a blogger, I literally pour my heart and soul into my writing. So, it's a bit disheartening when the audience doesn't match up with my passion.

That day was different. I noticed the stats were already in the hundreds. And every time I clicked "refresh," the views would continue to multiply.

"A fluke," I thought to myself. The only time I've ever had stats like these was when a much more seasoned blogger shared my posts. This only occurred when I would send the blogger a load of encouragement to read my posts. The thought of one of my posts having an organic growth the size of Texas was nothing more than a pipe dream.

But, it wasn't a fluke. By days' end, the views were in the thousands, and the momentum was just getting started. In just four days' time, I had over 300,000 individual views of "Dear Joey". Radio stations and other bloggers were sharing the post. It was all over Facebook, Twitter, Pinterest, and many other social media platforms.

Even now, several months later, people are still reading "Dear Joey". I realized, soon after, that maybe people do want to hear what I have to say. Not only that, but the world really, really loves Joey Feek.

So, this book is for you, dear reader. It's written because one woman dared to face life with a smile on her face. She smiled through the pain, through the uncertainty, through the trial she was handed. We can learn so much from her.

And that's why this book exists.

dear joey,

Last night you changed my life.

I don't even know you, and yet, you spoke a thousand things to me in a single picture.

I regret to tell you, that I've never heard your music. I had, honestly, never heard of you before last week. I guess I wasn't paying attention. I hope that doesn't offend you.

So, my intentions in writing you this letter, before you see our Savior, are as pure as gold. I am not seeking to bask in the shadow of your celebrity.

I'm writing you because I, like millions of others, saw the photo of you cuddling your toddler baby in an article last night.

dear joey,

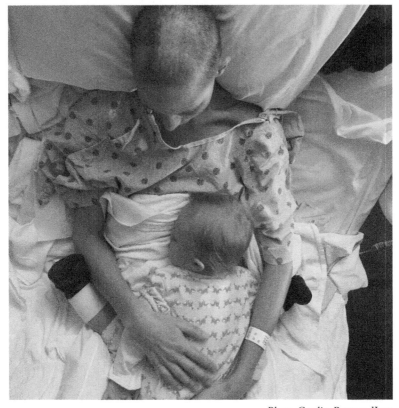

Photo Credit: RoryandJoey

I stared.

I just took the whole beautiful tragedy in over the course of several minutes.

I wept a little thinking of how you are doing exactly what we should all be doing as mothers: seizing the time we have left.

Because, really, we all know deep down that these lives are just as changing and fragile as the leaves. I've lived this year fearful, anxious, panicked, and depressed. I've had some minor health issues, but nothing like what you are currently enduring. And yet, I've lived as though there was no hope. I'm embarrassed by that.

You reminded me that while you are very fragile and filled with excruciating pain, that I am not, and I've chosen not to live life like I should.

You reminded me that the present moments we have are all that we truly have, and that gift of "next breath" may never be breathed.

You showed me that I should be thankful to still be able to make meals, chase my toddler, and carry the endless loads of laundry because I am able to do so. I'm sure I would miss that if it was taken from me. I can only imagine you would love to do that for your family right now. And I bet you would make them the most delicious feast, and the smile wouldn't leave your face.

I can't remember the last time I smiled while making dinner.

I bet you wouldn't grumble about folding tiny pink clothes before your sweet Indy throws them all across the room. The laundry game that almost every mother can relate to.

I know you wouldn't turn down "just one more book" or that glass of water before bedtime because there can never be too much reading and serving, really. You've reminded me that the "just make it until bedtime" mentality is an outlook that doesn't welcome the mess-making and joy-filled chaos.

And so, you've ruined me. And I'm glad you have. I

needed the ruining; the realization that these family times are the best of times.

Joey, I don't know exactly what you're feeling at this moment, but know this: you are still doing the hard work of motherhood. You're teaching all of us that motherhood is beautiful in all stages, even when it's time for motherhood to end.

I will be praying for you and your family in the coming days, weeks, months, years. I hope your daughters can always somehow experience the love you have for them, even from afar.

And I will always remember that you taught me more from a picture than any book, blog post, or mom friend could ever gift me. To love each messy, crazy, motherhood moment and to live fully in each breath.

Until we meet,
Alicia

Embracing a New Day

*"Openin' the windows and lettin' in air, holding hands
when we're saying a prayer. That's important to me."*
—Joey Feek, "That's Important to Me"

It's 6:00 a.m.

The three-year-old begins yelling the baby's name: "Em-mmmm-mmmaaahhhh."

I toss and turn as the voices in my head get louder and louder. Sometimes, dreams can be so cruel.

Suddenly, my dream seems more real than ever, until I finally realize: "This is really happening. Those are my girls' actual voices and that clock really does say six, zero, zero."

As my brain continues the boot-up process, mimicking the speed of the most primitive desktop computers, I feel like shedding a tear. My brain tells my eyelids to open, but I remind them that I'm in charge.

"Not now," I say to myself; "don't they know what time it is?". As I succumb to my fate, I quickly realize that the same amount of darkness is filling the room as was at four hours prior when I went to nurse the baby.

Sigh.

Cringe.

Wallow.

"Maybe they'll go back to sleep. Maybe if I ignore them, they'll stop their pointless chatter and realize they've been sorely mistaken. The sun has yet to crest the horizon. Today's home-school lesson will surely focus around this concept."

But, they don't stop. In fact, that pointless chatter has now made its way into the room across the hall. With the addition of the whispers coming from the children in the other room, the 6:00 a.m. pillow talk sessions begin to feel like fingernails on a chalkboard to my already overloaded senses.

I try to desperately channel my inner Peter Pan and "think happy thawts", but the only thought I can string together properly is, "I'm done. I haven't even started yet, and I'm already d.o.n.e."

Good Morning?

The least favorite thing I do every day is wake up. Somewhere between moving to the country, surrounded by trees and shade, and having baby number five, I began to hate mornings.

During college, I was a morning person. During night waking, in the wee early days of motherhood, I was like "give me all the babies." It didn't faze me. I never wanted help. I never woke my husband, and I always loved to see those rays of sunshine blasting though the windows at 7:00 AM.

But now, I wonder if those space movies are legit. The movies where a crew travels ten light years away and they're forced to sleep in those super cool capsules the whole way in order to conserve energy, rations, and other supplies. I'd totally hop into one of those "sleep for two years straight" capsules. I have even considered starting my own mission to another galaxy, full of sleep-deprived mothers only. If you want a ticket, I promise I'll save you one.

The second least favorite thing happens immediately following my least favorite thing: the making of the breakfast. As I fight with myself the entire way down the hall, my steps more automatic than deliberate, I wrack my brain over what to make for my ravenous crew. Despair, annoyance, and frustration rears their ugly heads in place of clear thought. Certainly, not the best combination to meet head-on with five vibrant "Good Mornings!" and a handful of breakfast suggestions each.

"Good. Morning.," I shoot back to each of them with the most half-hearted smile I can muster.

"No, we're not eating Pop-Tarts. They're gross."

"But why, Mommy?"

"Carter, you cannot steal the whole plate of bacon. Hunter, please help your sister clean up her spilled milk. Great, we're out of coffee."

By the time that everyone is fed and cleaned up, I'm ready for a nap. Forget the home-schooling studies. Forget dressing myself and applying a bit of light makeup. I have zero will to brush my hair, either. Forget it all. I'm hardly ready to tackle the next thing, much less go make pillow forts with pre-schoolers for the next two hours.

When the cloud of motherhood is thick and foggy, it's hard to embrace a new day with singing and sunshine. I usually find myself just waving my arms frantically trying to push back the thickness in those first hours of the day.

Do you ever feel this way?

A New Song

Does your outlook on each day seem to dictate how and if you will fully embrace motherhood?

If so, then I completely understand how you feel.

Unfortunately, approaching a new day with bitterness in our hearts is not what God intends for us to do. God wants us to embrace each day as the gift that it is, and fill the day with songs of praises to Him.

"Sing to the LORD, all the earth; proclaim his salvation day after day."
—1 Chronicles 16:23

"Come, let us sing for joy to the LORD; let us shout aloud to the Rock of our salvation."
—Psalm 95:1

"But I will sing of your strength, in the morning I will sing of your love; for you are my fortress, my refuge in times of trouble."
—Psalm 59:16

"Let us come before him with thanksgiving and extol him with music and song."
—Psalm 95:2

I'll be honest with you and say the last thing I want to do in the morning is sing praises while cereal bowls and juice-filled cups are being spilled every forty-five seconds or so. Instead, I'd like to remind Jesus that while I'm here cleaning up messes I didn't make, that His call to worship in these moments seems a tad unreasonable.

In fact, the following verses seem to speak a bit deeper to me in these moments:

"Evening, morning and noon I cry out in distress..."
—Psalm 55:17

"All day long I have been afflicted, and every morning brings new punishments."
—Psalm 73:14

There. Those verses are more like it. Every morning does seem like a new punishment. Every sunrise feels like some sort of cruel reminder that chirpy birds and cheerful children await my bitterly exhausted body.

A Heart Like David

If we look more closely at the verses I shared, we should remember that, more than likely, David was the author of them all. If we know anything about David, it's the fact that God called him a "Man after His own heart". David's heart was running after God, even when his emotions weren't. His writings remind me of a very hill-filled roller-coaster ride. We find so many valley moments of him crying out to God in despair and confusion, followed by times of the purest praise and the acknowledgement that God is unchangeable. And yet, God used his story and struggles to arguably make him the most quoted Biblical author.

Your praise and your sorrows can both, equally, be given to God. He can handle anything you throw His way. Even when you're caught crying over spilt milk.

A Changing Perspective

When I first found Joey's photo, it was like having all of the air punched out of me. Never had my heart felt so naked and exposed before. (Well, besides when Jesus exposed my sin and my need for Him.) Within seconds, I quickly came to realize how incredibly ungrateful I am for the life I've been given. Truly, I have nothing to complain about. I mean, hearing the cheerful chatters of little children in the morning is hardly a decent example of torture.

I began to search the depths of my heart. The harder I searched, the more disgusted I became. I realized that my "lemony-sour" attitude each morning reflected nothing about the Hope that I possess. It gave no clue as to the Truth I claimed to follow, or the example I meant to set for my children each day.

Instead, I met each day feeling defeated before my feet even touched the ground. It's as if I could almost see Satan smiling at me. My curt replies, sneers, and scowls towards my husband, because he was leaving me to face another day of motherhood, alone, made him feel both unappreciated and unloved. I was inflicting wounds on our marriage. Those infection-filled wounds left their mark on our marriage. All the while, Satan was having a hey-day with our family.

Comparison Stole My Joy

When I focused on the fear that would breed throughout my day, I felt as if my mind was rapidly becoming victim to the quicksand that is anxiety. By days' end, I could literally feel Satan laughing his head off at me. Another day was essentially wasted. Another day had been taken for granted, filled with untrue thoughts, and marked by both shameful actions and reactions. I was busy developing a habit I had no idea would be so hard to break.

In our social-media-saturated culture of the "highlight reel", it's so very easy to mindlessly scroll through the photos and statuses of our friends and family members while harvesting a growing weed of jealousy. I found myself scrolling through Facebook and Instagram feeling like life was being lived all around me. Like I was being left behind. Didn't anyone care?

I was reminded, via my little sister, that what I see on social media is nothing more than a "highlight reel". When I saw other mothers taking selfies of their Target trips with their loose curls and skinny jeans, latte in hand, I tried to remember that I was seeing just one piece of the puzzle. After all, we rarely photograph the meltdown moments, and the days we fail to run a comb through our hair.

Regardless of the friendly reminder my sister gave me, I still found myself fighting with my social media use. Most days, even now, I find I still do a decent amount of fighting.

Being a stay-at-home-mother can be one of the loneliest callings in the world. We mothers tend to overwhelm our husbands at the end of the day, and speak an average of twenty thousand words in a matter of minutes. After all, toddler and baby conversations aren't exactly the type of socialization we're missing here. Plus, it's exhausting to get out for playdates on the regular. Packing sippy cups, strollers, bags, snacks, blankies, and other life-saving supplies, just to meet a friend at the park for an hour seems excessively daunting to a mother running on forty-five minutes of sleep.

So, naturally, most of us use social media as our one connection to life that happens beyond our own walls. When we do this, our minds will fill with images of what we've seen and heard. If we aren't careful, we can allow those things to penetrate our hearts and leave us with an attitude of self-loathing. A habit of feeling like we aren't "enough". And if you find yourself currently there, you know it's incredibly almost impossible to remove yourself.

We must get into a habit of doing those things that will encourage us to embrace the day ahead. That may look slightly different for all of us, but there are a few things you must do each morning to welcome the gift that is today.

Meditate on Christ

The best, first thing you must do each morning is to have your mind immediately go to God. Let Him be your first thought. The best part is, you don't even have to move in order to do this. Just lie in bed for your first five minutes and focus on His goodness, His love for you, and the enormous amounts of grace that He has prepared for you, for this day. Maybe just allow a few "Thank You's" to leave your lips as you ponder His never-failing goodness.

Next, allow your thoughts to be consumed with anything and everything that describes Him. This sounds so easy, in theory, but it may take some strict discipline. I know most of our first impulses in the morning is to grab our phones and begin working out our thumbs. Truthfully, your thumbs get enough of a workout during the day as it is. So, make the hard choice to not reach for your phone upon first wake.

You may envision this time as something more. If so, get up, grab that cup of coffee or tea, and sit with the Word in hand. Devote whatever time you can, allowing Him to fill you up for the day.

I know not all of us can do this. So many of us are in the thick of mothering the full twenty-four hours in a day. You may have a new baby and the idea of waking up earlier to have time to read and pray may not be for you in this season. That's okay. Don't allow Satan to fill your mind with guilt over it, if you don't feel up to it. He's rather good at making us feel guilty for all the ways we don't quite measure-up in our motherhood journeys. Don't fall for it. Which leads me to my next point.

Remember God's Promises

This is such a simple exercise to do, also, while still in bed. Focus on these verses, memorize them, go to bed replaying them in your mind, or write them down on paper and be crazy enough to tape them to your ceiling. You'll have no choice but to see them when you wake up. Here are some of those verses:

God Promises Eternal Life:

> *"And this is the promise He has promised us—eternal life."*
> *— 1 John 2:25*

God Can Do the Impossible:

> *But He said, "The things which are impossible with men are possible with God."*
> *—Luke 18:27*

God Provides:

> *"Oh, fear the Lord, you His saints! There is no want to those who fear Him. The lions lack and suffer hunger; but those who seek the Lord shall not lack any good thing."*
> *—Psalm 34:9-10*

dear jocy,

God's Wisdom:

> *"Trust in the Lord with all your heart, and lean*
> *not on your own understanding; In all your ways*
> *acknowledge Him, and He shall direct your paths.*
> *Do not be wise in your own eyes; Fear the Lord and*
> *depart from evil."*
> —*Proverbs 3:5-7*

God's Peace:

> *"Great peace have those who love Your law, and*
> *nothing causes them to stumble."*
> —*Psalm 119:165*

God Will Help With Temptation:

> *"Therefore submit to God. Resist the devil and he will*
> *flee from you. Draw near to God and He will draw*
> *near to you."*
> —*James 4:7*

> *"For in that He Himself has suffered, being tempted,*
> *He is able to aid those who are tempted."*
> —*Hebrews 2:18*

God Can Remove Our Fear:

> *"I sought the Lord, and He heard me, and delivered me*
> *from all my fears."*
> —*Psalm 34:4*

God Has Conquered the Grave:

> *"And God will wipe away every tear from their eyes;*
> *there shall be no more death, nor sorrow, nor crying.*
> *There shall be no more pain, for the former things*
> *have passed away."*
> —*Revelation 21:4*

This is just a small sampling of the thousands, yes, thousands of promises you can hold tight to. Satan doesn't want us to remember God's Promises. He wants us doing life just like I had been: feeling grumpy, defeated, and stressed out.

What happens when you feel that way? Do you get much accomplished? Do you feel like meeting the needs of others, or praising God with your life? Of course, you don't! When you wake up in the morning, counting the promises of God, Satan is stopped before he can even begin. You have the upper hand. You can dictate how you will approach this new day. Don't give the Enemy the power he *doesn't* have over you!

Embracing Change

*"Progress is impossible without change, and those who
cannot change their minds cannot change anything."*
—*George Bernard Shaw*

My father was and still is, a big tease.

It used to drive me nuts, as a child and teenager, when my
dad would tease, tickle, and pick on me. He always did it out
of love. He was such a fun and silly Dad. I was just ultra-se-
rious and he had the most fun exposing my fake attempts at
being super-reserved and proper.

My mother would always remind me that if I didn't react
so dramatically, he wouldn't pick on me so often. To him, it
was the most fun game in the world.

I remember, as a teen, saying to my mother, "I hate it
when dad...(enter annoying moment here)" and she would
always reply with "Your father is (enter current age here)

years old. He's not going to change."

I hated it when she said that. For one, I always thought, "So what, my dad is somehow unchangeable?". It never occurred to me that maybe he didn't actually want to change. I still hated her excuse for him, though. Since I was his daughter, was I immune to change as well? Apparently, deep down, I thought so.

But, change is my friend. If it's my idea, of course.

The Daydreamer's Curse

Any daydreamers out there?

That's me. I grew up obsessed with Disney's animated Cinderella movie. According to my mother, I would watch it about every single day. She said I could quote along with the movie at age two. My favorite line was, "They can't order me to stop dreaming!". Certainly a line us dreamers can always identify with. And, of course, I always loved the song "A Dream Is A Wish (Your Heart Makes)", because, who doesn't like that song? I sing it to my little girls now, several times a week.

But, unfortunately, I think a curse comes with being a chronic daydreamer. Chronic daydreamers tend to be some of the most easily disappointed humans. It's really hard for us to accept that "life-is-hard-and-mostly-unpredictable" part. Feeling disappointed is painful. Constantly feeling like life and your dreams aren't lining up just right, is very frustrating.

I've had to realize that change won't ever come and seek our permission to walk thru the door. It won't knock softly and wait until you're ready to open the door for it. It won't even knock, usually. Change just barges in like a burglar, chaotically stealing all of the wishes Cinderella said we could keep. And, good grief, I trusted Cinderella.

Embrace it. Embrace that change will come. Plan for it. It doesn't have to sneak up on you. Just expect to be disappointed sometimes. Life is very disappointing. Christ does tell us in His Word to expect trouble. He tells us that trials and tribulations will come:

> *"I have told you these things, so that in me you may*
> *have peace. In this world, you will have trouble. But*
> *take heart! I have overcome the world."*
> —*John 16:33*

Not If, But When

Change is painful because we don't like change. We like to sit in the same seat, in the same row, in the same section at church. We like to use the same bathroom stall, sleep on the same side of the bed, use the same coffee mug every day. There's no doubt that we are creatures of habit. In fact, most changes are downright painful.

The pain change causes us doesn't have to stay painful. Instead, we have the ability, through Christ, to turn change into opportunities for wisdom.

Sometimes God takes us through times of drastic change. We go kicking and screaming like a toddler, because, how dare He try to move us! Fear of the unknown seeps in and it gets very comfortable. And speaking of comfortable, fear loves to keep us comfortable where we are. But, instead of fearing the change, we should fear the comfortableness that comes with staying where we are.

You Have Trust Issues

It's all about trust.

When you peel back the onion that is the fear of change, what we are truly afraid of is trusting God. And those of us who have issues trusting, also have an issue with control. We're always the ones who must drive, pay the bills, hover near our children screaming "be careful!" every five seconds while they attempt the monkey bars. We can't stand to not be in control. We want to drive our minivans with little to no speed bumps. Just open highway. Life is good.

Life can still be good. In fact, it can be infinitely better once we realize that: 1) We aren't in control, and 2) God can see the future, and we can't.

So, if He knows, and we don't, then why do we stand stubbornly in our little mud pie while God is trying to tell us that life is so much better over where He is?

I don't know very many people who have ever "arrived"

in this area of trust and acceptance for change. I truly believe that embracing change and our lack of true control, is the battle of our lives. But, wouldn't you love to just take Christ's hand and journey with Him? Stop fighting. Allow Him to do His work in you. Even if it is painful, remember that Christ makes beauty from ashes. He is the Potter, not us. We are His clay. We are the medium He's chosen to use to spread His truth to a hurting world.

If He uproots you from your job, your dream home, your relatively comfortable lifestyle, to go, do, and be something or go somewhere where His plan is bigger, then you go and do that thing. If He takes something valuable to you away, praise His name anyway. Be thankful He always knows better than you do.

When I consider Joey, I'm certain she had her moments where she wrestled hard with God in the quiet. She may have struggled understanding why would God allow her to go through the hard road she found herself in the middle of. It's something, I'm sure she would've never chosen for herself. It's also something that if I knew the road He was about to take me down, there would be no way I would've allowed Him to do the driving. Nope. We're pulling over. Which is exactly why He doesn't allow us to know the future.

I know for a fact, He never left her to walk it alone. I know that the beauty of worshipping an omnipotent God is that He doesn't always owe us an explanation. In fact, I believe, with all my heart, that in these moments of uncertain trial, God desires us all to default to just blindly trusting Him. In all our trials and tribulations, the safest conclusion for our one-million "Why"s is "It's for His good and His glory." Period. Any explanation beyond that really isn't necessary.

Whether you're fighting a heart change, a physical change, a location change, or a job change, put your trust in the One who does not change. Don't wrestle Him. Instead, rest in the fact that God will always carry you through the change, and that not being open to change is what you should ultimately fear.

Nobody Else Can Do the Changing

Have you ever had a list of things that you wanted to change, but never did? Your weight? Your eating habits? Your schedule? The way the laundry just does its thing and you're its favorite victim? Maybe it's the way you wake up every morning and you just automatically want to pull the covers over your head.

I had these issues and more. They would plague me every single day and I would just sit and cry and wallow, "Why can't just one of these things just fix itself?"

After months of living this way, I realized something quite profound: "These things aren't gonna get fixed on their own."

If you want something to change, you'll have to change it

yourself. Nobody is going to do the changing for you.

The same goes for God. God isn't going to be constantly in your face, pushing you in a stroller towards the next step in life. He wants you to walk with Him. He wants you to make the choice to change. He gives us the power to do all the changing we need, through Him.

As a blogger, I strive to share candidly. I'm not afraid to be completely real with my readers. If you read my writings, it won't take long for you to essentially know everything about me.

I'd like to end this chapter with an old post I wrote that has to do with accepting and embracing the will to change our lives:

If I Can Be So Honest...

"This morning, I sobbed.

As I watched my husband drive slowly down the driveway, I just sat in my own puddle.

It didn't matter that I had my favorite latte patiently waiting for first sip. It didn't matter that it's Friday, or that I finally had a night where I didn't cough the entire time.

After my uncontrolled emotions decided they'd had enough of a tantrum, I got up.

Normally, I wouldn't have gotten up. I would've remained in my depression. But that, I've noticed, hasn't served me very well.

So, I sent the kiddos outside to "beat the heat" and I turned on Christina Aguilera (Old Christina, to clarify). I decided to get busy.

I've been sick this week. And I've been trying to work out for the past 2-3 weeks almost every day. That's unheard of for me.

In fact, one year ago today, I was a blob.

A skinny blob, but a blob no less. I spent most of every single day in my husband's brown chair. I had no energy. I couldn't eat enough. I lost weight by breathing.

I was at rock bottom. I literally longed to die. I would daydream about it. Yet, it terrified me all the same. If it wasn't for my best friend driving over twenty minutes to my house every day (for the record, I never asked her to, that's just how amazing she is) and my other best friend loaning me her 15-year-old on Wednesdays, I think my children would've had to raise themselves. It was that bad.

I quickly developed this mentality that I don't deserve happiness. That I was to become a martyr to Motherhood; to life. I also believed that Christ desired me to stay in the valley with no hope of gaining the strength to climb back out.

I thought He wanted me to stay in the belly of the whale. And it's been super hard to break free from that lie the enemy *planted in my heart.*

In fact, up until a couple of weeks ago, I wholeheartedly believed that I didn't deserve much of anything good. That the goodness in my life had passed. I believed that I would just have to buckle up and stay on this motherhood ride until it ends eventually.

I thought "if I act happy, then people won't know how badly I'm hurting. Plus, it'll be fake and I'm not fake."

Its affected everything. My relationships. My book writing. My businesses that I long to be successful at. Everything.

I don't think my choice to exercise was what sparked a little change in me. I think it was the fact that I realized that if I want to change; If I want to see a different something in my life full of somethings, then I must do it. I do.

Hating oneself is a deadly poison. And, I can't quite tell you why I hated myself so very much. But I think it had something to do with being my own worst enemy.

Maybe you're in the thick of that right now, yourself. Maybe you feel like I did, and sometimes still do feel that everyone else deserves happiness except for you.

Maybe you believe a thousand and one lies like I did, and find myself still doing.

It's a hard process, no doubt. I have a long way to go, myself. But, first of all, if you have Christ, greater is He. And if you

dear joey,

have a will to change, those two things are all you need.

After that, purpose to make small opposite choices to what you've been doing.

I'm not an expert on this subject. I just know what I've learned. And I always want to share it with you. Vulnerability equals strength. Don't ever forget that.

And strength is only one choice away."

Embracing Joy

"Joy is distinctly a Christian word and a Christian thing. It is the reverse of happiness. Happiness is the result of what happens of an agreeable sort. Joy has its springs deep down inside. And that spring never runs dry, no matter what happens. Only Jesus gives that joy."
—S.D. Gordon

Your wedding day.

A new baby.

A job promotion.

Receiving that bit of good news, you've been waiting for.

Getting an unexpected amount of money.

Waking up to realize that your baby slept through the night.

All of these things seem to describe moments of joy. Moments of elation and encouragement. Moments where you just want to freeze time a bit and revel life's goodness.

But dare I say that none of those things bring true joy? What we're actually feeling is called happiness. Happiness is situational. Happiness comes and goes as often as the tides.

Happiness can leave as quickly as it came. One minute we could be ready to throw in the towel and then we get that phone call or witness that moment that we've been waiting for, and suddenly, the world is a right again. But, that isn't joy.

Joy Isn't a Feeling

I bet if you thought hard about it, you may have some trouble thinking of a person in your life that possesses true joy. I know I do. We tend to overwhelm our minds with replays of our circumstances and feelings; leaving no room for joy to enter in.

The truth is that joy isn't something that comes and goes easily. Joy is a state of mind. Joy is only found in one place. Joy is a person.

When Jesus said to take up our cross and follow Him, it sounds like the most unappealing invitation out there. I mean, who lures people into following them with a statement like that?

Well, Jesus did. And it was and still is the most welcoming invitation you will ever receive. Let me explain.

This is where it gets tricky with joy. Because you would think that taking up ones cross and dragging it along following an invisible, to us, man would be pure drudgery. Surely, this isn't where joy is hiding. Surely this couldn't be what Christ had in mind for our "abundant life" He promised!

Jesus' brother James stated that we should "Count it all joy…when you fall into various tribulation." Paul said that he, "…joyed in his sufferings."

How is it even possible for these men to suggest, both of them multiple times, that there is joy found in suffering for Christ? It seems counterintuitive if we only look at it from the surface. So now, we must go deeper.

Christ suffered more than any other human has or will ever suffer. When we invite Him into the home of our hearts, we have the ability to connect with Him on a level that transcends human explanation. Only this understanding doesn't bring about any sort of fleeting happiness, nor does it bring any hint of negativity.

As we draw nearer to the heart of Christ, something incredible happens. We begin to understand that everything that we thought filled our happiness cup pales in comparison to what He offers us in the way of joy.

Joy Only Comes from Christ

Once we learn that joy is only found inside of a deep relationship with Christ, we will then understand how we can do what James and Paul spoke of in those verses concerning joy in suffering. We will realize, that because joy is a steady rippling brook of life for our soul, our sufferings aren't able to overwhelm us anymore. They are just simply an extension of Christ. They are opportunities for us to go even deeper into our understanding of Him. They are gifts to us instead of a scourge. They are vital to our growth. They give us a visual of how mighty and limitless God really is.

When we realize that joy can only be found in Christ, we will stop searching for it everywhere else. We will then put all of that energy into furthering our understanding of Him. The amount of joy He offers to us is overflowing and abundant. We will no longer lack for anything. We have the opportunity to stop the pursuit of happiness and drink deeply from the well of joy.

It's Complicated

Like everything else humans twist and skew, staying joyful is one of those things that we tend to muddle. God made it simple for us: if we keep our eyes on Him and we keep His Word at the forefront of our minds, then we will absolutely live joyfully. No exceptions.

Unfortunately, we make it complicated. We get distracted. And like a treasure hunter in search of the finest gold, we search for joy and peace in everything but Christ. We love to fill our lives with temporary highs, always longing for that next opportunity to leap into happiness or drown away our sorrows. We avoid struggle, we buckle under the pain and pressure, and when things get bad, we shake our fists and claim injustice. We beg for mercy, pray with swelling eyes for peace, and long for comfort when things don't go our way.

We think that we can control and pilot our own lives without God's help and then once we run out of gas and the plane starts to crash, we frantically scramble to call for His rescuing.

The moment we choose to realize that Christ is enough, is the moment we are choosing joy. Is Christ enough for you? Is He really, truly enough? I may venture to say that most of us would answer with a shameful "No". The pursuit of Christ is the highway to a joyful life. Seeking Him to get something in return won't work. Seeking to strengthen your relationship with Him, while treating Him like your personal genie, won't work. On the surface, it's great that you are willing to develop a constant dialogue with Him, but it won't satisfy us if we keep speaking while seeking. The pursuit of Christ, himself, just realizing that He is the enough that we're longing for, that's when joy makes itself at home in your heart.

Nothing can steal that joy away from you, unless you choose to walk away from it. No amount of temptation, hardship, or struggle can snatch the joy from your life. Here are some promises concerning joy that you can store in your heart:

*"Go eat your food with gladness, and drink your wine
with a joyful heart, for God has already approved*

what you do."
—*Ecclesiastes 9:7*

"*The prospect of the righteous is joy, but the hopes of the wicked come to nothing.*"
—*Proverbs 10:28*

"*Though you have not seen him, you love him; and even though you do not see him now, you believe in him and are filled with an inexpressible and glorious joy, for you are receiving the end result of your faith, the salvation of your souls.*"
— *1 Peter 1:8-9*

"*May the God of hope fill you with all joy and peace as you trust in him, so that you may overflow with hope by the power of the Holy Spirit.*"
—*Romans 15:13*

"*So with you: Now is your time of grief, but I will see you again and you will rejoice, and no one will take away your joy.*"
—*Jesus, John 16:22*

Choosing Joy

Since joy comes from a series of choices that make Christ

enough; every moment, we should be in the habit of choosing that joy over anything else. Yes, we have options. And no, Christ won't make us choose what He knows is best for us. That's completely up to us.

You must wake up every morning and choose to say, "No matter what occurs today, Christ is my 'enough'". If my children run me ragged today, it's fine, because my hope is not found in how they behave. If I wake up sick, and all my plans for the day are ruined, it's fine because God's grace has met me here and joy can stay in my heart.

"...for the joy of the Lord is your strength."
—*Nehemiah 8:10*

I have this placard that I bought at Hobby Lobby on clearance. I placed it on the shelf beside my back door. It says "Choose Joy". What it should say is "Choose Christ". Because, with every thought, with every action, we should always seek Him. There is no substitute for the joy He has waiting for us when we do.

four

Embracing Bedtime & Grace

*"Bedtime: The perfect time for kids to ask questions,
need the toilet, want some food, need a new night-
light...or anything else, other than sleep!"*
—*Unknown*

I know what you're probably thinking right now. Why
should you even bother reading this chapter after reading
the title? After all, I think all mothers, everywhere, have no
trouble embracing bedtime.

I'm with you on that one. I have no trouble either. Except,
I do.

For as long as I can remember, I've always been extremely
"non-flexible" when it comes to my children's bedtime. Some
families I know work on a more "night-owl" schedule than
my family does. I've always been somewhat in awe of those
families.

However, we have always treasured our quiet times after

the children are in bed, and so an earlier bedtime has always worked for us. Up until I had our fifth child, I was a stickler for the 7pm infant bedtime. Toddlers go to bed no later than 7:30, older kids go to bed no later than 9:00. We would completely avoid activities after dinner or cut activities short, just to strictly accommodate our bedtime routine. Life would stop as bedtime neared.

I was, and still am, very strict about no children sleeping in our bed. Newborns and young infants are welcome to cuddle and nurse all night long, but once the child is no longer a small baby, we prefer to go to them and comfort the child in their own room.

Children with bad dreams? We go to them, comfort them, pray with them, and then hopefully everyone is back to sleep. I never believed in any cry it out methods. Despite our restrictions, we usually have great experiences at bedtime and throughout the night.

But, I've noticed something. When bedtime creeps around the corner, so does my sour attitude. It's the attitude that rushes, snaps, and sighs with relief when children are tucked safe in their beds.

I may hear a thousand "I need a drink's" and "Can you read me that story?"'s. Usually, I'm always annoyed by it. I sigh, I grumble, I snap, I say "No" before they can finish their sentence. My flesh takes over, and I just wish away the demands and the sheer overwhelm of those moments. After all, can't they see that I'm tired?

A Cup of Cold Water

I always feel that little prick on my heart when I snap, grumble, or sigh. I know where it's coming from. I've been pricked a thousand times before. It's always a gentle prick, but it still stings a bit. And it always, always gets me to think. This verse inevitably comes to mind in these moments:

> *"And whoever in the name of a disciple gives to one of*
> *these little ones even a cup of cold water to drink, truly*
> *I say to you, he shall not lose his reward."*
> —*Jesus, Matthew 10:42*

I quickly take my own inventory and try to turn things around. As I walk down the long hallway to our kitchen, I begin to count my blessings. The marvel that is running water coming out of my refrigerator, the blessing that is walking, the fact that my child is safely and snuggly in her warm bed, waiting for this water. I mean, the humbling can be quite hard to swallow.

Reluctantly, I apologize to my child. I realize that asking for their forgiveness is just one of those very tough parts of parenting. A ritual that I find myself doing more often than I intended I would when I set out on this parenting journey.

What They Wouldn't Give

It's tough not to justify the selfishness in our hearts when bedtime comes around. I mean, we have been doing the hard work of parenting all day long, typically with little to no breaks. There are no re-enforcements, no tag-teaming, no real companionship in this motherhood endeavor. And, when the final hours creep up, we just do all we can to make it to that finish line where we close the door behind us and release a huge sigh.

Typically, after the bedtime drama is complete, I take a second inventory of how I could've handled those moments better. This time, I consider the other mothers I cannot see.

I think of the mother that may be overseas serving our country. What she wouldn't give to breathe in the scent of her freshly bathed little ones, and to kiss them sweetly on the forehead as they drift off.

I consider the mother who may not be physically able to tuck her children in, grab the glass of water, or read that last story again and again. Whether she is experiencing a sickness, is in hospital, or cannot physically do those things she longs to do as a mother, it makes me feel horribly that I allowed my attitude to take those things for granted.

I focus on the mothers that may long for their child in the night. The mothers who wish that they could just have one more embrace, one more lullaby, one more gaze at their child's beauty. The mothers who find their hearts in heaven and their bodies on autopilot.

I also think of the women who long to have my life. The women whose greatest desires are all found in the gift of motherhood. The gift that never seems to come.

My mind finally goes to those children who are motherless. The children who will never ever know a mother's touch, the sweet symphony of her songs, or have her wrap them up in their favorite blankie.

The bottom line is, maybe we should slow down instead of speed up during the night hours. Maybe we should stop only seeing our children as "sweet" while they're sleeping and notice how sweet and innocent they are while awake.

We're all exhausted by day's end. The struggle is so real. We have every right to be tired. We have every right to feel our frustrations are justified. Mothering is hard! But God's grace is greater. And we can pour out that grace, especially as bedtime draws near.

Consider This Grace

God is our Heavenly Father. He is the ultimate parent. The only true parenting expert that exists. He parents billions of His children, all day long, every second of the day, with no breaks. Yes, of course, He doesn't need a break, He's God, after all. But, He does understand what it's like to be bone tired, because He became a man through His Son, Jesus. He does understand motherhood, because He created it. You can't create something and then not understand the product you created. It wouldn't make sense.

I used to consider that God didn't know anything about motherhood because He has never been a mother. He doesn't know what childbirth is like, He has no clue about hormones, breastfeeding, getting up twenty-five times in the middle of the night, or hearing your own name called hundreds of times a day. He couldn't possibly understand me. He's clueless about these things. Right? Wrong.

The truth was that I was believing a lie straight from the Master of Lies, himself. God does understand all those things I mentioned about motherhood, plus more. He gets it. He does understand you. He does long to help, encourage, and lift you up when you feel like you're drowning.

> *"For from His fullness, we have all received grace upon grace."*
> —John 1:16

Just enough.

For today only.

We usually make sure we have enough for our tomorrow's. According to God, that represents a lack of trust. I know I try to busily gather enough of everything for tomorrow, but Christ never suggests that we do so. In fact, He doesn't even want us considering tomorrow at all.

No Hoarding Allowed

Consider the Israelites for a moment. In the midst of their time in the wilderness, God provided their daily sustenance. Food literally fell from the heavens every day, at the same time, in the same manner. The only rule that God gave them was that they weren't allowed to gather enough for the next day. And on the sixth day, they could gather enough for both that day and the next, which was the Sabbath.

> *"So the people of Israel did as they were told. Some*
> *gathered a lot, some only a little. But when they*
> *measured it out, everyone had just enough. Those who*
> *gathered a lot had nothing left ober, and those who*
> *gathered only a little had enough. Each family had just*
> *what it needed.*
>
> *Then Moses told them, "Do not keep any of it until*
> *morning," But some of them didn't listen and kept*
> *some of it until morning. But, by then, it was full of*
> *maggots and had a terrible smell. Moses was very*
> *angry with them."*
> —*Exodus 16:17-20*

Why wouldn't God want them to gather as much as they possibly could and then meal plan for the week? What's wrong with putting our extras in Tupperware containers for tomorrow?

God knew His people. He knows us, too. He knows that if we begin to hoard today for our tomorrow's, then we will inevitably begin to rely on our own plans and abilities rather than His own.

God knows that while being smart about the future is wise, living in those tomorrow's is not. He desires for us to be fully present now; completely reliant on Him for today's, and only today's, provisions.

He gives us just enough.

He does. Just enough for today's "everything"s. Enough endurance. Enough hope. Enough sustenance. Enough grace. Enough mercy. Enough. Not an abundance so we can spill over into the next weeks' mishaps, but enough for right at this moment.

Why? Because He wants us. He wants our attention. He wants us to breathe Him in and exhale anticipating the next inhale, because He loves us that much. He is so crazy about our well-being and longs so much for us to understand Him, He designed this life in such a way that just five minutes of navigating on our own feels like we're sinking the ship. Yet, we constantly take over and raise the white flag when things get too difficult.

Just be here now.
Just be.
Here.
Now.
With Me.
And breathe.
Allow Me to feed you what you need. I already know
what you need. No. No. Don't keep filling your arms
with these loads. Put it all in my hands. Just keep

allowing me to provide. You keep your eyes right
here. Don't move. This is where you thrive. I Am your
manna.

Grace Enough to Live

I never knew Joey in real life. Although, I feel like I knew
her for years. She lived under the umbrella of God's im-
measurable grace. Which is why it seemed she lived life so
effortlessly, up until her final moments. Even at the brink of
death, her life was beautiful. The bulk of her beauty came
from understanding and living in God's grace.

We have two choices when we accept God's free gift of
salvation through grace. First, we can live life like a martyr.
We can choose to be a victim to life and its uncertainties,
just longing and waiting for the rescuing that God promises
His children. Or, we can live life with the purpose He gifted
all of us. We each have an active purpose for His Kingdom,
and it's your job to actively seek Him for Him to reveal that
purpose to you. He will reveal it, in His perfect time.

Will you be ready for the "revealing"?

five

Embracing Servanthood

"For who is the greater, one who reclines at table or one who serves? Is it not the one who reclines at the table? But I am among you as the one who serves."
—Jesus, Luke 22:27

Sometimes I think that motherhood and servanthood are synonymous. Really.

Every time I have to fill in one of those applications where they ask "occupation", there's usually always a "home-maker" option. For years, I've been tempted to cross that option out and write the word "servanthood". Or, at least express that I'm in the business of doing the same things, day in and day out, all for other people, without any sort of compensation.

There's this annoying consensus amongst a group of rather intelligent humans that believe that motherhood is living on easy street. That it's somehow filled with pillow filled, cozy mornings, snuggling in bed until 10AM, while little children quietly play at their mother's feet with books and sweet, little wooden blocks. They think that some magician comes in to fold laundry and make organic homemade breads all day while the mother goes out to frolic in a field nearby, spinning her toddler in circles, as they bask in the sunny breezes.

Whoever thinks such things has been watching way too many commercials.

I wish I could take those misinformed humans and give them a thorough glimpse into what a day of servanthood, rather motherhood, looks like. I think we can all agree that most of those spectators would at least leave us with a hug, an apology, and maybe a basket of folded laundry, if we're lucky.

Jars of Clay

> *"But we have this treasure in jars of clay to show that this all-surpassing power is from God and not from us."*
> —*2 Corinthians 4:7*

Think about a clay pot for a second.

How would you describe it?

Hand-made.

Fragile.

Unique.

Purposeful.

Empty.

Filled.

Pieced together.

From the earth.

Christ compares us in Corinthians to these jars of clay. As jars of clay, we can hold treasures of truth for the world. But sometimes, our pot cracks and breaks. Sometimes, we need a little gluing back together. Sometimes, we stay high on a shelf and don't find ourselves useful at all, collecting the dust of life. But, sometimes, we discover we are filled to the brim with life giving waters, being passed from one person to another, filling souls with hope as they deeply drink from our vessel.

It's funny to me how Christ chose to use our jars of clay as the catalyst to further His kingdom. How fragile and unreliable we are. How incredibly ineffective we can be. Why didn't he choose the angels to spread this life giving message of the Gospel? After all, they did a fine job of announcing His birth. The sky was illuminated with their beauty, the message was heard loud and clear, truly fit for the King of Kings.

And here we are, likened to a vessel that is so vulnerable to living creatures. We are at the mercy of the Maker both in the creation and using of our vessel.

We are made to be used. We have great purpose given to us by the great Jar Maker, Himself. Motherhood and servanthood will always be synonymous, and our jars will need to be continuously refilled with fresh water, as we are being poured out, daily.

The Least of These

> *"Pure and genuine religion in the sight of God the Father means caring for orphans and widows in their distress and refusing to let the world corrupt you."*
> —James 1:27

> *"Let the little children come to me, and do not hinder them, for the kingdom of heaven belongs to such as these."*
> —Jesus, Matthew 19:13

I look at these verses and my heart desires to immediately take on the responsibility found in them. I know that, as mothers, we are called to do just that; to open our hearts to the least and the lost.

I know from experience, that it's so easy to feel harried in the thick of motherhood. We tend to overwhelm ourselves with how "put together" we appear to everyone else. All the while, the real purpose we have, is found somewhere under that pile of Pinterest crafts we have never gotten time to finish.

I wonder how different life would be if we only cared about what God thought of everything. I bet we'd find more time to do the things that matter to Him instead of all those "must-do's" that we consider critical. Our calling as mother's can be reduced to the simplest concept: servanthood. Most often, we are too busy to even look up to notice that there is an entire world beyond our little niche that needs help. Our first responsibility is found at home. Serving our families is priority one. Being in constant service to our husbands first and foremost, then to our children. But while these are priority, we must redeem the time we've been given to include the outside world into that "serving" as well.

What can you plan to do today, this week, this month, for the world found beyond your walls? How can you actively serve those in your community and beyond?

It could be something as simple as a phone call to someone that you have lost touch with over the years. It could include running an errand for your grand-parent, or taking flowers and a meal to another mother who is sick. If you find yourself struggling with what you should and could physically and financially do for others, just ask God. Tell Him that you have a willing heart to help and serve in His name, and then just wait for Him to pile on the opportunities.

Besides Paul, James is my favorite Bible character. The amount of humility he possessed to refer to himself as a servant instead of the brother of Christ is overwhelmingly amazing to me.

Here is a blog post I wrote on James:

James, A Servant

"Each day, homeschooling five little ones is never easy. But, it's become my normal and is typically always this beautiful chaos of sorts. Then, rarely, I have days like today where it's seriously one mishap after another to the point where I almost should laugh when just one more thing goes crazy wrong.

[Picture two massive blowouts from two of my daughters, a middle daughter whom I watched from afar as she gently poured my completely full cup of room temp {because I never got a chance to partake} coffee on her lap as she lazed about in the recliner, a sliced middle finger courtesy of my apple corer-slicer, and a puddle of juice on the kitchen floor all while trying to give my older sons their math tests.]

Life never stops. Especially here. And even though it's far from quiet at quiet time right now, I sat down to read anyway. My plan was to read the book of James before reentering the chaos of serving my children today. But I can't make it past the first sentence: "James, a servant of God and of The Lord Jesus Christ."

This same James who was the real-life brother of Jesus doesn't begin his writings with the recognition that he was blood related to The Christ. He never even mentions his relation. Instead, he refers himself as a servant of God, a servant of his brother, Jesus Christ.

Humility. Beyond my comprehension. I'm always taken aback when I read his humble introduction.

He's a servant. How much more should I be a servant? Motherhood is serving. And days like today remind me that serving my home and my family isn't always fun. It isn't always filled with beautiful creativity, sweet smelling kitchens and lap-reading snugly times. Serving others, serving our families, and serving our Creator is stretching and exposing and full of both joy and tears.

Serving one another is what this life is all about. Never are we more like Christ than when we serve. And never am I more humbled than when I am reminded by James that we all are just humans and none of us should be elevated except for to elevate the God-Man that came to serve and be served, Jesus.

And then we must "Consider it pure joy, my brothers, whenever you face trials of many kinds, because you know that the testing of your faith develops perseverance. Perseverance must finish its work so that you may be mature and complete, not lacking anything."
—James 1:2-4

The Purpose Behind the Trouble

"...just as the Son of Man did not come to be served, but to serve, and to give his life as a ransom for many."
—Jesus, Matthew 20:28

Have you ever heard that quote, "If it's good enough for Jesus, then it's good enough for me!"? I love that quote, but then again, maybe I don't love it that much. Because, well, Jesus didn't live this fabulous life full of amazing possessions, beautiful vacations, and free from ridicule. In fact, Jesus didn't live any sort of life that we should be envious of. I don't know of many of us who would choose to be born in a filthy barn and placed into a slimy, smelly feeding trough to sleep as an infant. Nor do I suspect that many of us would choose to be born into poverty, a life doing hard labor, and being constantly chastised and ridiculed by his peers and family. Imagine being the only perfectly behaved one out of your siblings? Imagine always being right, never needing correction and living in and amongst sinners at every turn? Imagine knowing the exact moment when you would die? Imagine knowing and understanding what all this ridicule and hate would lead to? Imagine loving these people despite knowing the deepest, darkest parts of their hearts?

I marvel at the fact that the God that spoke all of life into existence, came down, made himself an embryo, lived life amongst us all and called Himself a servant of men. He, the God Man, did not come to be served by us, but to serve us instead. Incredible!

It's an incredibly, mind-boggling thing to swallow. Truly. How much more then should we be servants to one another? We are not above servanthood. Quite the opposite.

We should, instead, be rabid embracers of this thing called servanthood.

Let's face it, some people are just too difficult to serve. They don't appreciate anything. Instead, they seek to capitalize on your servanthood, almost expecting more. Some are literally offended when others seek to serve them. Remember, to not take offense when this occurs. It has nothing to do with you, but everything to do with their heart condition, which is more than likely filled to overflowing with pride.

No matter what, we must embrace servanthood because that's exactly the example that Christ left us with. Even encouraging us to go so far as to be willing to die for one another. To be a servant takes true sacrifice. But, the sacrifice is worth it all because it inevitably leads us closer to Him.

Embracing Suffering

"The tiny seed knew that in order to grow
it needed to be dropped in dirt, covered in
darkness, and struggle to reach the light."
—*Unknown*

Metamorphosis

Have you ever witnessed a freshly-formed butterfly emerge from its cocoon? I have. It's beautifully frustrating. To be audience to that kind of struggle, my instinct was to just reach out to help. It took forever. Yet, I knew if I helped, the helping would equal a sure death sentence for the metamorphed creature.

Witnessing this process, made me realize that the metamorphosis that it went thru for several weeks was the "easy part". Breaking free from its prison, however, was not. But, in case you weren't aware, those are the very moments where the butterfly gathers all the strength it needs to face its new life.

Another example would be the tiny sprout. So fragile, and yet entirely strong, as it pushes through the blanket of soil that once covered it.

One Seed Per Hole

Three years ago, my husband and I started our first modest garden. We had little clue as to what we were doing, and because of that, made some huge novice mistakes.

I recall my husband staring at these seeds the size of a sentence period, and concluding that you must need to put 3-4 seeds per hole for there to be any chance of a decent harvest.

Little did he know that our tiny 3x5 foot garden would yield over three hundred tomatoes that summer. We couldn't pick them or consume them fast enough. We gave so many away, it was hilarious.

We surely won't ever make that mistake again. One seed per hole. One. That's all it takes for a tiny speck of potential to turn into a bountiful harvest.

Growing Pains

Growth doesn't happen without growing pains. The struggle, the fragility, the dependence on the roots, the soil, the water, the air, the sunlight; these things must be in place or the harvest will never come. Some of us are in that time of struggle right now. Desperately trying to remove ourselves from a time of change. Desperate to escape and fly onward. But the change must occur, the struggle to be free must take place, or we won't have the strength to keep going.

Others of us are in that growth phase, completely reliant on the pouring into that may come from others. Some of us are just waiting to be fully ripe so that we can nurture and sustain others on their journey. And it will come.

The harvest always comes.

It's no wonder that the process of life always follows the struggle. Butterflies, babies, fruit: all emerge after a period of rapid growth, change, and lastly, the struggle of their lives.

Wherever you find yourself in your journey, may you seek to find the beauty in the struggle, because it's there to make you stronger. I know this from experience. An experience I've both come to equally love and hate at the same time.

That Time That 2015 Was Terrible

The year 2015 can easily go down as the year that was out of control. Well, only out of my control, that is. I suppose every year before that year could also be described as such. Maybe, because the years' prior, the years when I thought everything was going my way (aka. The years I didn't rely on God so much), weren't. It was just an illusion of control.

I have these moments every month where life just seems

too big, sounds that reach over a whisper make my teeth cringe, and I can't find any good reason to get out of bed except for the fact that I have no other option. On one of these days, in particular, I found myself with an old stethoscope trying to listen to my own heartbeat as if I was qualified to do so. I was trying to find an arrhythmia, namely atrial fibrillation, because I was convinced that I was experiencing it. My heart was racing and my mind was going at NASCAR speeds to keep up with it, all the while the sounds of five joy-filled voices filled the next room over. I had been audience to another anxiety-ridden woman who suffered from the actual atrial fibrillation. Like, she had it on her medical chart, had been diagnosed by a doctor, and had solid evidence to go by that this did really exist in her world. Me? Mine was just a fabrication.

"How weird are you?!?" I thought to myself. "Here you are, beautiful spring day, hormones raging, using a stethoscope, and are worried about dying again!! When, in the next room, life abounds in the most blessed ways, and you can't see past your 'crazy' to just hang it all up and join them!!!".

How to Live in Fear 101

Anxiety came crashing into my world at the end of January 2015. My first panic attack was in a Michael's craft store, in the check out, with five, very young, but very well-behaved children. I didn't know what I was experiencing, at the time, was a panic attack. In fact, I really had no solid knowledge of what anxiety felt like prior to this moment. Come to find out, I had been a horrible hydrator of my body. I had previously gotten away with eating late, meagre lunches and drinking maybe twice a day for so long, that it never occurred to me that maybe I should change my habits. Years of constant nursing and pregnancies kind of caught up with me after I turned thirty, and now my body was about to show me what an internal temper tantrum was like.

As I stood in that check-out lane, I was about thirty seconds from my turn, but I was also feeling like I was thirty seconds until I passed out on that cold, hard, stark white tile. I calmly put all of our crafts to the side, told the most well-behaved and forgiving children on the planet, that I was sorry, and walked out.

I had no clue what was happening, so naturally, I panicked some more. I attempted to drive home, but my heart was racing around 180bpm and I figured that it was poor judgment to attempt a ten-minute drive alone with my most precious cargo. So, I turned around and went back to the same Michael's shopping center parking lot to the Urgent Care nearby.

The fear was building in my mind as my heart wouldn't obey my commands to just calm down. I kept the van running and got out without unbuckling my children. As I peeked my head inside the waiting room, I called to them that I needed help now, but my five small children, including my five-month-old nursling, were still in the vehicle. They immediately took me back, and hooked me up to an EKG machine to take my heart rhythms. One of the clinicians went out to remove my children from the vehicle and brought them inside to the waiting room. My husband was on his way, but he was almost forty minutes away, and couldn't make it there fast enough. Meanwhile, an ambulance was called and I nursed my baby one last time with tiny tears streaming down my face.

The ambulance ride was almost unbearable. I had to hear my heart beating quickly the entire time, as if feeling it beat that quickly wasn't enough. I kept thinking of my children over and over again. I had never, ever been away from them before. I never missed a day of their lives prior to this moment. Except for one day, when my third baby was in the NICU for three weeks. I missed one entire day of her life because I didn't have anyone to watch our sons so I could visit her. It was horrible.

When I arrived at the ER, they tried all of their traditional, medicine-like attempts at getting my heart to obey. It wouldn't. It never did the entire weekend. I was an emotional wreck.

I was transferred, three days into my stay, to another, much larger hospital in the heart of my home city. The same hospital that I had given birth in four times before. The hospital that I remember only experiencing joyful things in.

I was scheduled for an ablation procedure during an electrical study on my heart. While I was in that procedure, the doctor found that my ablation couldn't take place because the extra electrical pathway they found, sits one millimetre on top of my original electrical pacemaker.

The good news was; my new diagnosis wasn't fatal. It was more of a nuisance than anything. I can live with that. Right?

Wrong.

After that entire four days was over, I felt totally traumatized. The fear that gripped my heart was intense, and I allowed it to dig its roots in deep and strong. Over the months that followed, I breathed in fear and exhaled anxiety. I lost thirty pounds almost instantly. I didn't understand why. I thought it was these new supplements I was taking, or that I was drinking a lot more water than I'd ever had before.

By the time April and May were here, I was begging God to take me out of this life. I had no idea what was wrong with me. I was filled to the brim with anxiety-depression, sapped of all of my energy, I would daydream about my own death. I all but super-glued myself to the front porch rocking chair, and would sit, sometimes up to 6-8 hours rocking all day while watching my children gleefully embrace their life with me in standby mode.

Head-On Collision

Then came a brick wall. Our medical sharing group refused to cover any of my medical bills because this diagnosis was a "pre-existing condition". For nine solid months, we fought, we sought physician's letters, we went into major debt, and had more arguments in those few months than we had in our entire marriage combined.

Every single month, I would lose all of my energy for several days at a time. I would end up on the ground, unable to move, struggling to breathe. My husband would be called home countless times to "rescue me" and pick up where I had left off with the children. My closest friend made it her mission to drive thirty minutes to my home each day and care for our, combined, nine children ranging in ages from eleven to twelve months (For the record, we had two brand-new one year olds in that mix).

I later would discover, after a score of additional doctors' visits, a handful of prescriptions for anti-depressants and anti-anxiety medications, and vials upon vials of bloodwork later, that the medicine they so graciously gave me to calm my heart in the ER back in January, had given me thyroid disease. The extreme, sudden weight loss, the boughts of extreme anxiety and depression, and my episodes of complete and total fatigue and lethargy; It all made sense. I discovered this in September of that year, and was told then that it would clear up on its own, after seeing an Endocrinologist.

Equipped with new information, a sense of frustration and relief washed over me. "If only I hadn't even gone to Michael's that January afternoon, I wouldn't be dealing with any of this right now! I wouldn't have to see my husband so intensely stressed about my health, my medical bills, my ability to even function enough to care for our brood every day." I still didn't feel myself, and I was just as confused as before, on how to get back to what I thought was normal. I began seeing an amazing chiropractor. I know, for a fact, that this was the second vital step in my healing. Not long after I began seeing him regularly, we got a call we never thought would come. Our medical sharing group had decided to pay all the medical bills I had accrued in full. Paid in full. I couldn't believe it. Things were finally turning around. No more arguments. No more stress, upon stress, upon stress.

It's All Under Control

When I look back at that year, I try to see the whole puzzle, not just the pieces that make the puzzle. For the first time in my life, I saw clearly that, God wanted me to cling to Him. He's been wanting me to cling to Him all along, I was just too confident, in my own way, to notice.

If there was one thing I wish the world would know about Christ-followers, it's that a lot of us are busy going our own way, but we cling to the label we have no intention of living up to. Christ-follower, "Little Christ's", that's what Christian means. I would have that label gripped tightly in my right hand, while walking my days without merely a thought of Him.

Recently, while having one of my "nervous" days, I was crying and asking God, "Why now? Why do I have to deal with these stresses, fears, anxieties, health issues now, with five children, sixteen chickens, a husband, and while averaging fifteen loads of laundry a week?" He reminded me that He allowed me plenty of time, years, in fact, to navigate motherhood on my own. I fired back with "wasn't I doing just fine?"

I thought about it. I did do just fine. I kept up with it all. I got up every single time a baby cried in the night. I nursed all of my children for at least a year or more. The thought of taking four children to Target on a Tuesday morning didn't intimidate me. I laughed in my heart at the mom's that could barely handle their one or two children in the store, while my children always behaved immaculately. Nothing "motherhood related" intimidated me.

Sleepless nights, grocery shopping with children all around me, and a 1400 square foot house with a steep flight of stairs and several wobbly toddlers couldn't break me. I despise the term "Supermom", but that's exactly what I was. Aside from life's regular hiccups, everything was under control. My control.

I did the most awesome baking activities, crafts, lessons, and experiments. We had nightly dance parties, I would match their outfits, we went on field trips, tackled traffic and parking garages downtown, we helped others, and surprised friends with little gifts of love all of the time.

I was doing a good job. Actually, a great job! My children knew the love of Christ. I would teach them, read to them, pray with them, show them the way to heaven is through Jesus. And God has used me as the one to lead them all to Him, so far. Each of those moments are permanently sewn into my heart.

And then, all of this happened. Right when things were starting to get really tough. Right when our stress levels from moving and having a new baby the year prior were still super fresh. The year 2015 was where suffering met up to sweep the rug out from under me.

I still find myself trying to smooth it out so that I don't trip on it as I walk. Full of fear and anxiety, I have avoided the field trips, I could care less about the crafts and experiments, and the dance parties are just a memory now. So I asked God, quite bluntly, actually, and with ample amounts of emotion, "Why do I have to deal with all of this now? Why not when I had less responsibility, less children to care for, and when I lived closer to our parents?"

I waited.

About ten minutes later I heard that voice that flows like a river. He said, "Alicia, I let you do it your way long enough."

"But didn't I do a good enough job? I was doing just fine relying on my own strength."

Sure, I'd include God, in my days, here and there. I would, like any good Christian, have a steady stream of quiet time and devotion for several weeks and then, like a magicians' illusion, those times would vanish. This happened in steady cycles, every few months. Devotion. Closeness. Distraction. Comfortableness. Conviction. Another cycle of devotion. Repeat. Over, and over, and over again this occurred. The only time I really found myself clinging to God was when my third pregnancy ended a bit too soon and my first daughter, the daughter I had diligently dreamed about and prayed for, for years, was in the NICU for three weeks.

"Yes, you did a great job," He said to me, voice as calm and steady as a gentle breeze, "but you didn't need me, and I love you too much to not have you needing me. You must accept the consequences of your actions now. You drove yourself too hard for too long. You didn't care for yourself, both physically as much as spiritually as you should have. You made motherhood your god, and never quite understood that motherhood is a dance between the two of us. You forgot to include me."

The tears began to flow as I finally understood why I had to be broken. I was too invested in my own strength. I thought I was immune to suffering. I thought I was invincible. He reminded me, and continues to remind me, that I'm not.

Every day, for months, I've suffered with my thoughts, my anxieties, my physical weakness, trying to navigate, by process of elimination, what will and won't work to get my physical body to somehow return to its former glory. More importantly, I now cling, daily, to my God. I have no other choice. He loves me too much to allow me to rely on myself any more.

Victoriously Suffering

Maybe that's you, today. Maybe you sit and ponder, "Why me? Why now? Why this?"

God doesn't owe us an explanation, unfortunately. After all, some of His ways will forever remain mysterious to us. But, what I do know is, that He promised us there would be suffering to be endured while here, but to keep our eyes on the victory. It was one of the main points He carefully emphasized prior to His death.

"I have told you these things, so that in me you may have peace. In this world you will have trouble. But take heart! I have overcome the world."

—*John 16:33*

"Let us not grow weary in doing good, for at the proper time, we will reap a harvest, if we do not give up."

—*Galatians 6:9*

Praying for Suffering

My little brother, at the ripe old age of twenty-four, told our father one time, that he prays for suffering. My father asked him "Why?", and my brother responded with, "Because it keeps us holy and dependent upon God."

Wow. Think about that for a moment. Actually, to this day, I still chew on that and think, "I'm so not there yet. Will I ever be?" Praying for suffering seems so absolutely ridiculous in our culture of comfort.

I look at the way Joey Feek just seemed to beautifully embrace the road of suffering she was on. To us, as her audience, she never seemed to display bitterness or frustration. She chose to embrace the life she had been given, even while she was bound to an uncomfortable hospital bed. She knew that the world was watching her. She understood that while life can be extremely unfair and unpredictable, God forever remains good.

We Can't Flee from Suffering

I don't know about you, but to me, motherhood is the most heart-wrenching, soul-exposing, and holiness-making journeys we will ever have. We can't go at it alone. And, we can't fight the suffering parts. As much as we desire to flee the scene of our suffering, there is no greater treasure than to stop and notice God in the midst of it. To see His face, filled with love and adoration for you as you parent His gifts. To remember that in the middle of the storm, all we have to do is keep our eyes on Him and we can walk on water, too.

One of my favorite passages in the entire Bible is Matthew 8:23-27:

*"Then he got into the boat and his disciples followed
him. Suddenly a furious storm came up on the lake,
so that the waves swept over the boat.But Jesus was
sleeping.*

*The disciples went and woke him, saying, "Lord, save
us! We're going to drown!"*

*He replied, "You of little faith, why are you so afraid?"
Then He got up and rebuked the winds and the waves,
and it was completely calm.*

*The men were amazed and asked, "What kind of man
is this? Even the winds and the waves obey Him!"*

How easily we can apply these verses to our own lives!
The sacrifice of, first acknowledging His sacrifice for us,
then choosing to follow Him, and finally stepping into the
boat (of our lives) with Him. The first moments our life
begins to rock and rattle from the intensity of the waves we
encounter, we panic. We look around, frantically searching
for Him. "Why isn't He freaking out with me?", "Why can't I
hear His voice?", "Where is He??".

But Jesus isn't freaked out. He won't yell over the commotion.
He is still in the boat with you. He hasn't left your side. Even
though some of us will ignorantly "jump ship" anyway.

Curl Up With Jesus

How many times have you frantically waved your arms up
at God, screaming, "Hey! Down here! It's not going so well!

Do something!!!"? All of us may feel this way at one time or another, but Christ isn't up in some cloud, sipping lemonade, while watching all of His children down here suffering for His sake. This isn't His free entertainment. Instead, He's right there in the midst of the trouble you find yourself in. He may even be sleeping, because He knows that there's nothing to worry about. If you're sharing a boat with Him, really, what have you to be concerned about? What we should do, instead, is realize that maybe the best solution is to walk over to where Jesus is resting and curl up next to Him while the storm rages around you. God certainly can calm every storm in our lives, but sometimes He chooses not to. Sometimes, we just need to hunker down and sleep beside His peacefulness, knowing that we are safe in His care.

I want to close this chapter with this blog post I wrote at the height of my struggle with anxiety, depression, and panic. It's one of only two dreams I've ever had that felt like complete reality.

"Rest, My Daughter"

I want you to picture Jesus in front of you now.

Allow the reality of Him being in the flesh, you in His overwhelming presence, and all of the potential emotions that come with that encounter.

Picture His eyes as He gazes on you with an intense love

we can not duplicate elsewhere. Imagine the peace and comfort that radiates from His body towards your soul.

You see His eyes begin to glisten as He understands and knows fully well the pain, the exhaustion, the weariness you've been carrying.

He calmly suggests, as a tear or two falls from His eyes, to "Come. Rest."

You begin to weep, as you release all of the burden you've chosen to carry alone, onto His lap.

He doesn't speak, but gently wipes your tears away with His garment, and strokes your hair with tenderness.

He has all of the time in the world for you. He doesn't rush you. He doesn't have anywhere else He must be. He doesn't mindlessly check His iPhone, or think ahead to what He should eat for dinner. He just allows you to rest.

He stays perfectly still so as not to disturb you. All the while, He never thinks to look up from watching you sleep.

And when you awake, He is still there. Still watching you. Still comforting you. He is ready to listen, ready to heal, ready to watch you rest all over again, if that is what you choose to do.

All of our sorrows, anxieties, troubles, negative thoughts, hurts, pains, confusion, and overwhelming "everything's" can and will disappear in His presence (If we allow).

He never gets a cramp from you resting too long on His shoulder; He never wants to see you leave His side. And, yet, we always (eventually) do.

We get up, tell Him thank you, and walk away towards everything that we hate. Back towards the pain. Back towards the aloneness, the confusion, and the lies we believe more than the truth He gifts to us.

He hates to see us go, but He never makes us stay.

He never leaves that spot, dear daughter. He never leaves that place. He stays put so you can find Him once more, right where you [shouldn't] have left Him.

Each time, you are greeted with both a smile and tears. "I've missed you," He says, with the same loving tone you've come to both crave and doubt.

He's never condescending, never judgmental, never projecting a "know-it-all" attitude towards your ridiculously poor choice to leave Him once again.

He's there. Present. Ready to comfort, and heal, and lavish you with His perfect love once again. You simply just need to turn around.

He wipes your tears and you rest once more. He knows you won't stay long, and it hurts Him to think you will soon leave again, but for now, He sits. You have some resting to do. And there's nowhere else He'd rather be.

"For only those who believe can enter His rest."
—Hebrews 4:3

seven

Embracing Life at Home (and Beyond)

*"We need to learn this secret of the burning heart.
Suddenly Jesus appears to us, fires are set ablaze, and
we are given wonderful visions; but then we must
learn to maintain the secret of the burning heart—a
heart that can go through anything. It is the simple,
dreary day, with its commonplace duties and people,
that smothers the burning heart—unless we have
learned the secret of abiding in Jesus."*
—Oswald Chambers, My Utmost for His Highest

Martyr.

Like Paul, the martyred missionary for Christ endured
endless hours and days in a prison, rotting away. Day in, day
out, he had the same routine. Trapped. Longing for anything
other than another opportunity to stare at a stone wall for
hours upon hours. Wishing. Hoping. Praying for the chains
to be removed from his hands and feet.

Adjustment Curve

Motherhood can feel eerily similar to a prison. Maybe not exactly like the prison Paul was in, but the isolation, the mundane repetition, the feeling of being trapped, those are all very real.

I'll never forget the day I felt trapped in motherhood. I was two weeks in and feeling like an incredible failure. Just eighteen months prior, I was moving out of my dorm room for the final time. I was so used to constant interaction. Constant conversation, noise, laughter, and fun consumed my days. Our dorm room was a literal revolving door for the rest of the girls on our hall. My roommate, and best friend at the time, had this magnetic personality that literally was likeable to every person she came within breathing distance of. People were taken with her. I was her slightly intro-verted sidekick, but I thrived in the environment we had created for ourselves.

When marriage began almost immediately after I handed in my dorm keys, I had a bit of an adjustment period living in such a quiet atmosphere. I was already used to the "sharing spaces" parts of it all, but living with a male human was a totally new experience.

It wasn't long before God gave me another male to share spaces with. Our first-born son arrived seventeen months after we said "I Do". He was colicky for the first three months of life. My days of new motherhood were spent trying to keep my son from screaming most of the day. Not at all what I pictured my motherhood would be.

Each day passed as slowly as trying to squeeze honey out of a jar. I seriously contemplated contacting Gerber and Huggies to inform them that their warm, fuzzy little advertisements about motherhood were highly deceptive and misleading. I felt like I had been lied to. Where were the sweet giggly bath time moments? Where were the quiet, cuddly sleepy moments? And for goodness sakes, where was my baby hiding the "off" button?!?

Motherhood was some sort of cruel joke. And the joke was certainly on me.

Errands and a Newborn

One time, I got brave enough to run errands on a cool afternoon in late November. I had my little, teenage brother with me as a sort of support person. I don't know how much support I really expected my sixteen-year-old little brother to give me, but nonetheless, his "almost" adult presence gave me that extra boost I needed to get out with my two-week-old.

I knew my little bundle hated his car seat. So I made sure all the necessities were in order before gently placing him in his prison cell. With his diaper changed, full belly, comfy cozy clothes, and his favorite binky in place, we set off on our ten-minute drive to town.

It wasn't long before he got wind of where he was and

set out to remind us both how much he hated the current situation. The errands took all of thirty minutes, maybe, and when it was time to place him back into the car seat for the short ride home, all hell broke loose.

I barely made it an entire mile down the road until I quickly swerved into a random neighborhood on my left. The sobs and wails had reached an epic-ness I have since yet to encounter again in any newborn child.

We both exited the car and I quickly removed my highly overwhelmed child out of the car seat. He was soaking wet. It was maybe sixty-five degrees out, at the most. Truly, a gorgeous fall day right before the busyness of Thanksgiving.

Drenched in his own sweat, he continued to sob uncontrollably. I thought, "This kid has seriously lit himself on fire! How in the world does this happen?". I ripped his clothes off, fanned him down, and pulled out every single soothing method I had in my brand-new motherhood bag of tricks. Nothing worked. I looked at my brother, he looked at me, quite helplessly, I may add, and I just put my hysterical son back into his car seat. The faster we make it back to the "safe zone" (home), the better.

I told my brother to get back in the car; that we would just hightail it home and do our best to ignore his misunderstood pleas. But no amount of volume increase on the radio could drown out his massive, newborn style meltdown. At that point, I could no longer hold it together, either. I began to cry along with him. I thought in my typical overly dramatic fashion, "I'll honestly never get to comfortably leave my house again. Motherhood hates me. My child hates me".

It was a long time afterwards until I felt confident enough to venture out into the world again with my child. I cared about what others would think if he suddenly started wailing like he did that day in the car. I cared about everyone staring at me. I cared about how silly and frazzled I would feel when I couldn't get him to stop. So, I stayed home.

I stayed home a little too much.

A State of Depression

I had some serious baby blues after little man was born, but nothing compared to the full-fledged onslaught of some major hormonal issues after those first weeks. When his colic set in, so did my post-partum depression. I didn't know that's what I had when I had it, until one day, three months after the fact, he stopped crying all day and so did I. It's like this massive cloud was lifted from my mind, and I noticed that I was still living and this was my new life. I don't even remember much from this time of new motherhood, thanks to the depression and his colic issues. A whole entire third of that year is a massive blur in my head. All I know was that it was borderline insanity. Each and every single day was just no sleep and lots and lots of tears.

My sweet husband would encourage me to take a break when our son was (finally) sleeping, to just recharge for a bit. I, idiotically, didn't take him up on his offer very often, if ever. I was determined that motherhood, no matter how unexpectedly cruel it had been to me so far, was mine to conquer. It's my job, not my husband's, to raise this baby to independence.

The Great Lie Detox

It didn't take long, after I got into the swing of motherhood, to start to feel sorry for myself. After all, there are so many injustices that come alongside new motherhood. First, it's hard to keep that whole self-pity thing at bay when one averages about twenty hours of sleep a week. The sleep-deprivation thing alone is enough to bring on the steady waterworks and make one question all the things.

Second, it's tough getting over the initial shock and awe that motherhood doesn't exactly, quite re-semble all those sweet Huggies advertisements you saw while your belly was swelling and you equated a poor night's sleep to getting jabbed in the side a few times at night. Goodness knows, when mother's feel tired, overwhelmed and puny, there may as well be a wide-open door for the Enemy to walk right in. And, that's precisely what he does. He just walks right in, and vulnerable us, we listen to his subtleness. Like the Wicked Queen in the fairy tale of Snow White, he hands us a shiny, red apple that looks too decadent to resist. He preys on our hunger. The hunger that is found in the trenches of sleepless nights and endless diaper changes. He waits for us to reach out and take the bait. Because new motherhood doesn't organically afford time to actively dedicate to a meaningful investment in God, it becomes difficult to remember that appearances have nothing to do with what is found on the inside.

Starving, you reach out to take the apple and partake of its lusciousness. It tastes amazing. Juicy, sweet, a little waxy tasting on the outside, but that's not a huge deal. It's been a while since you had an organic, freshly picked apple, and you don't bother comparing the subtle differences. You eat, you feel satisfied, and it felt so good to just sit and let your mind wander for a bit. After all, you're so tired. And sometimes, it's easy to forget about lunch, and sometimes dinner, too.

On the surface, you aren't aware that you settled. But, deep down, you know you could've had better. Satan may have reached out to offer you a tiny dose of bitterness against your husband. You consider just how annoying it has been to be the only one that hears baby's cries at night. You might even consider getting his hearing checked. Satan may softly whisper inadequacies as you compare your day's events with another woman's. He may have you see the importance of comparing your physical appearance to another, newer mother, who has somehow cracked DaVinci's Code of postpartum weight loss a mere six weeks after giving birth. Frustration settles in your soul; bitterness squeezes your heart.

If your husband walks in after a long day at work, you may choose to not kiss him back. He asks if there's anything wrong and you rapidly reply with a sarcastic "No". Before he even makes it to the bedroom to change clothes, you allow yourself to burst into tears, partly in anger, because, to be honest, life and motherhood just isn't fair. You may envy his paycheck, envy his free time and radio-listening abilities on the way to work. You may envy his business dinner or a weekend away for job training. You may take out your frustrations on him because while you're busy thinking of everyone else in this house, you realize four days have gone by without a shower.

I used to think that my attitude and my frustrations were to be validated and catered to because motherhood is so very difficult and time consuming. I used to think that my victim-like approach was to be justified. It took, until very recently, for me to remove the scales from my eyes. I can finally see that Satan kept offering me something that just slightly deviated from what I should be focusing on. Instead of calling me inadequate and a failure, he put other mothers in my view, the exact type of mothers that he knew would have me calling myself inadequate and a failure. Because I wasn't actively in the Word of God, it was very easy to forget the truth's of God's Word I had memorized since childhood.

Beyond Motherhood

I would encourage all of you, while you are busy embracing motherhood, that you also remember to embrace the living that can be lived outside of your homes. There's a whole world out there that is missing your talents and your gifts while you are busy giving your family the world. Truly, we are meant to live our lives in both realms. Maybe not equally. Maybe not even close to equally, but we still must never lose ourselves in the daily tasks that motherhood requires so much so that it causes us to lose touch with the ways God has gifted us to reach the world.

Joining a mom's group in your area is a great idea. Sometimes, just gathering up the courage to go to the playground, solo, with your sleeping baby, is perfectly fine. Truly, no seasoned mother would dare give you crazy eyes for it. We've all been there. Some of us are still in the thick of the loneliness even now. I know, for me, ten years later, I still have to fight it. I'm an introvert at heart, and while I love to travel and get out, I love home, a good book, and some quiet.

Develop Your Passions

All too often, when motherhood overtakes our lives, our dreams and passions usually go on a high shelf to collect all the dust. Motherhood is frustratingly fulfilling, but it's not all that makes you, you. In fact, mothers must work hard to hold tightly to those things that make us well up with purpose and hope.

If you're in that season where you've lost yourself in motherhood; the season where you can't even remember what your favorite color is anymore. Then please know that you are not alone. The monotonous tasks of motherhood do a great job of reducing us all to baby feeders and diaper changers. I remember going to bed many nights thinking: "What did I do all day? I changed ten diapers and fed my baby eight times, and...Wow, that makes me super awesome! Not."

It's hard to feel full of purpose when you may have gone from career woman to master diaper changer. Sometimes, when it was just my first born and I, just for fun, I would time myself during diaper changes. It's a game I used to play with myself to make me feel slightly more useful and amazing. When I would beat my previous world record time, I would celebrate for a few seconds while watching the look on my baby's face. I'm sure he thought I was a bit nutty, but at least I got some adorable smiles out of the deal.

The important thing is that you do something that brings back that passion. Do you enjoy creating? Writing? Reading? Journaling? Baking? Tinkering? Gardening? Sewing? Blogging? Encouraging? Some-thing else entirely? Whatever it is, carve out time every single day that you can, and do the things that you love. Don't make one thousand and one excuses. Just do those things. Make it a habit to take care of yourself. Nurture yourself; nobody else is going to do it for you.

The Truth Is...

Satan wants us to feel discouraged, tired, depressed, used up, and unappreciated. If he succeeds in those areas, then he's done a pretty great job of making an entire group of potential world changers stuck in their monotony.

With Christ, that's what we are as mothers, world changers. Some of us are perfectly fine with ordinary. That's fine, too. But, God does desire to do extraordinary things, through you, for His glory. It doesn't matter if you feel like you aren't "enough", with God on your side, and through His limitless resources, you can do the extraordinary. Even while changing diapers.

If Satan can get most of us mothers to feel unworthy, unloved, and uncared for, then he's keeping us from being effective in our homes and communities. Sure, we'll still accomplish things every day, but we'll do so on a sort of autopilot. Mothering on autopilot isn't what God wills for our lives. He came so we can have abundant life through Him! Motherhood, even in the trenches, can be filled with abundance if we keep Him as our purpose!

The Goodness That Never Ceases

I'm sure you've heard that popular phrase "God is good: all the time, and all the time: God is good!"

Well, it's one-hundred percent true. Even when motherhood betrays us over, and over, and over again, He is good.

When we feel like we've got nothing left to give, He is still good. And when life falls apart all around us, one thing never, ever changes: His goodness. So, when you're up for the seventh time at night to hush a waking baby, remember: He is good, and He is your strength. When your husband has to be away on business, and there is no relief to look forward to: He is your peace and your relief during those long days. When life pulls the financial rug out from under you, He is your Good Provider. When a child unexpectedly falls ill, He is still good and He is your healer. He is always the good we hold to in the bad moments of life.

By the Light of the Super Moon

Have you ever witnessed the beauty and awe of a super moon? A super moon is that rare event where the moon is significantly closer to the earth than usual. Because of its closeness in proximity, the moon appears brighter and much larger than usual.

We sometimes forget that the moon cannot create its own light. As we sometimes marvel at its beauty in a sea full of stars, we fail to remember that if it weren't for the sun, the moon wouldn't even be noticeable to us at all. Its purpose would be hidden, and its value greatly diminished.

Everything that shines needs a source. A candle is but a waxy mass unless you light the wick. A lightbulb does no good if it's in the box it came in. The moon isn't able to light itself, thus relying completely upon its source to fulfill its number one purpose: to light up the night.

What about you? Christ tells us that we are the "...light of the world". How bright is that light of yours? Are you plugged into The Source? Are you actively aligning yourself with God's Word, staying close to His Will, and finding ways to serve Him where you are?

If so, your light should be like a super moon. An event that is so beautiful and breathtaking that it garners national news. Keep your light shining brightly, but allow the Light-Giver to give you that spark.

eight

Embracing Marriage

"The only way love can last a lifetime is if it's unconditional. The truth is this: love is not determined by the one being loved but rather by the one choosing to love."
—Stephen Kendrick

My husband will tell you, he isn't eloquent with his words. He's a "facts" kind of communicator, as I imagine most men are. But, he looked me in the eyes one night and his words just flowed out like the most perfect stream. I found myself writing them on my heart as he spoke. I didn't want to forget a word.

"I feel badly," he began. "You made it so easy for me. I had this beautiful, godly girl love me. When I finally matured enough to notice, I knew I could love you right back. And so I did. And you're more than I could've ever hoped to have searched for. But I never had to search because you were just always there. You love Jesus so much, you are good at so many things, you're just amazing and I am so grateful for you loving me in the first place. I love you so much, it's insane."

To hear my man, who is a 'man's-man-of-all-men' kind of man, express himself in my native language (words), was a gift I shall always cherish. It came from a man that's stuck by my side for over seventeen years now. His words were without agenda, and weren't lacking in substance. He didn't stumble. He just spoke his heart.

Marriage is certainly not made up of moments like those. But, goodness, when they come, the whole welcoming committee is there to greet them. Life goes on. Bills pile, children interrupt (good grief, do they ever interrupt), work schedules bleed us dry, and marriage is sometimes just barely sizzling on that back stove burner.

Beyond the Love Language

If you're a Christian couple, and you've been around for more than five minutes, chances are you've heard of a little book called "The Five Love Languages" written by Gary Chapman. Next to the Holy Bible, this book is arguably one of the most widely read and discussed in the Christian realm. It has currently sold multiple millions of copies and been translated into forty-nine languages around the world. To say that it's kind of a big deal is an understatement.

Pastor's use the book for premarital counseling. There

are Bible studies inspired by it. It's become the "unofficial" gold standard for any Christian relationship. There are even resources on how to find out your child's love language. The premise behind the book is that all of us speak one of five love languages naturally. In marriage, usually, the husband's and wife's love languages don't match up. Understanding how your spouse gives and receives love best is the key to a harmonious relationship, along with God as the center.

I love The Five Love Languages book. I've read it through completely. I've taken the online love language quiz three times. I've had my husband do it twice before. I know his love language. I know my own love language. I know my children's love languages. And yet, I found that even with all that knowledge, and actively practicing that knowledge, I found myself exhausted and frustrated.

I challenged myself to develop a new outlook on acts of love. I purposed to notice and receive every act of love that my husband showed to me, even if it wasn't my exact love language. My love language is quality time. It doesn't serve me well because I have a husband that works more than forty hours a week. When that's your reality, there's not a whole lot of quality time going down every day.

I found I would only focus on the fact that my over-worked husband would spend more time talking on the phone doing service calls than he did speaking to me. I would discredit his love because I didn't want to find it in the water bottle he brought me every night before bed or the way he woke up a little early to get our baby so I could sleep.

When I took the "quality time" lenses from my eyes, I immediately began to see all of the tiny, mundane, yet, sweet ways that my husband showed me love every day. It was like my whole world lit up like that glorious Christmas Tree at Rockefeller Center. I started taking photographs on my phone of the little things I purposed to now notice. After I collected all my photos from the day, I realized, this man really does love me so much!

As time went on, I grew more accustomed to seeing love in everything he did for me. When he would run to the grocery store for me, I made sure I thanked him, instead of grumble over the fact that he forgot vegetables and bought bologna. When he would say, "Go get some 'Alicia' time", I wouldn't take it as he didn't want to spend time with me. Instead, I tried not to argue. I tried to see things as he did; he simply wanted me to get a break from life.

My love language is still, and may forever be, quality time, but now, I realize that I can receive love in all of the other languages, too, and still feel loved. Don't make the mistake of putting your love language on a pedestal. Don't make it the god of your marriage. You will miss so many opportunities to see the hundreds and thousands of other ways your spouse chooses to love you. It reminds me that marriage isn't glamorous, nor is it as simple as speaking each other's love languages fluently without a translator. No, marriage is messy, real, hard, and worth fighting for. It really will make all of the difference in improving your marriage. Just look beyond your love language.

A Role You Weren't Meant to Fill

During my college years, I made up for all the lost time I wasted not growing spiritually. Growing up, there wasn't any part of my life that wasn't Christian. Okay, maybe my dentist wasn't Christian, and maybe that one set of neighbors we had in the cul-de-sac house, but that's pretty much it as far as I knew. Going to college, that was just another extension of the theme my life had held thus far: Christian.

My first week of college life was as fun as it was terrifying. I remember being assigned to a Prayer Leader and then meeting with our hall's SLD's (Spiritual Life Director's) and thinking, "I'll never be like these girls". But, I was wrong. I grew more spiritually that year, than ever before.

By Sophomore year of college, I was seriously considering joining the Spiritual Leadership Team, but couldn't due to my prior commitments to the school's marching band. (Yes, I was a band geek, and I'm proud of it!)

The following Junior year, I decided I would forego the marching band and try out Spiritual Leadership. I became an SLD alongside my amazing best friend that year. We had the best year rooming together and ministering to these girls on our hall. Sometimes we'd be up until two or three in the morning just pouring into these girls, our sisters, and our friends. I realized that I was a true spiritual leader amongst my peers, something I never considered myself before. I was so fulfilled doing God's work on my hall. It wasn't always easy, but it was so worth it.

Meanwhile, my fiancée was three hours south of my college, working hard at his first career job after graduating from a local college. He was busy discipling a handful of close friends and acquaintances that he knew from both work and college. He would meet with these guys once a week or more and would share the Gospel while filling them with encourage-ment and wisdom. A few times, on my college breaks, I would come home and witness him in action. It was so inspiring and so very attractive. I knew I was getting the total package. He was the most handsome, amazing, loving, spiritual leader, "Everything-I-could-ever-want-and-we'll-never-fight-ever-kind" of man.

The hard truth about a long-distance relationship is, that when you have those rare moments when you're actually in the same space, there's a lot of agreeing going on. Meaning, you're so caught up in actually breathing the same air that you'll be cordial no matter what. The moral of this story is that you really, foolishly allow the butterflies in your tummy to make all of the decisions.

What I expected, after witnessing my soon-to-be-hus-band share his faith multiple times to these guys, looking all smoking hot while doing so, is that we would be this unstoppable force for God. I pictured us riding off into the sunset, all beautiful, hair flowing, Bibles in hand, a tropical beach, some horses, a lot of smiling, lots of children all around us, missionaries for Christ, coconuts in the trees. (There goes my daydreaming, again!) But, it didn't really work out that way. And, it kind of took me a long time to recover from the backlash.

The wedding went off without a hitch. My Cinderella themed wedding was a dream come true.

The Honeymoon was lovely. But, three weeks in and, shockingly, we were having a rather exciting conversation about laundry habits. He passionately echoed that his way was amazing and should be quickly adopted in order to achieve harmony. On the contrary, I emphatically made my case that no adoption of his laundry policy would occur and that he must realize that my ways are superior to his own. After all, I'd been doing laundry for myself for over three years now. He was watching his own mother do his laundry this very day, one year prior. Clearly, I was the laundry expert between the two of us.

This was just the beginning. As time went on, I became more and more disappointed in this whole marriage thing. I can blame it on my viewing of Cinderella too much as a child, but really, I've always had this daydream thing going on regardless of what I consume visually. Bills came, money went, the honeymoon kept getting further removed, and we were left with an album of our fairytale. Is this what life is?

Just a constant pulling and tugging? Because my arms were already tired.

I began to wonder who stole the man of my dreams. Where's that man that constantly bought me flowers and wrote me love notes? Where's that guy I would stay up late with and type for hours on AOL Instant Messenger? I can't believe he yelled at me over some laundry! We weren't ever supposed to fight. That wasn't in my head! That wasn't part of my daydream!

When life took over, and I was no longer in my "Christian" bubble world, I stopped nurturing my relationship with God. After all, I wasn't accountable to anyone anymore except myself and "Grumpy Laundry Husband". He sure didn't mind that we didn't read the Bible together. My "missionary husband dreams" were so squashed that the ooze left-over made me nauseous.

I made sure that whenever I did read my Bible, that I did so deliberately in front of him. "That will teach him," I thought to myself, "he'll feel guilty soon enough." When that didn't work, and my outright verbal plea's and coaxing's didn't work, I resorted to tears. Then, when our boys came along, I made sure I took on the role of spiritual leader. If he doesn't want to do it, then I will. And I did.

And I was wrong.

It seems ridiculous, but I based how loveable my husband seemed by if he spoke my love language and if he lived up to my personal expectations of him. One of those expectations being the Bible reader in our home. I didn't consider that maybe I was the one more in the wrong here. I was failing to respect my husband, all while putting myself in a position that God never intended I take hold of.

No matter how annoying it is that your husband doesn't live up to your expectations, or maybe, ultimately, God's expectations, it's not your job to make sure he does. Our flesh may automatically yearn to be helpful to our husbands in these ways. After all, what's wrong with a little reminder every now and again? But, we must remember what Christ said about married women:

> *"Wives, in the same way be submissive to your hus-*
> *bands so that, if any of them do not believe the Word,*
> *they may be won over without words by the behavior*
> *of their wives, whom they see the purity and reverence*
> *of your lives."*
> —*I Peter 3:1*

God doesn't give His daughters permission to nag and belittle their husbands into salvation. Nor do we have the authority to do the same to our believing husbands who have yet to step up as Spiritual Leader of the home. If you have been behaving towards your husband in this way, I'd like to ask you, "How is that working out for you?". Really. Is he pleasantly responsive and immediately repentant? Chances are, the answer is a big, fat no.

Because our husbands thrive in an atmosphere of respect,

our "helpful" words and reminders that they aren't living up to their Godly duties, unfortunately, won't turn things around. What we should do, instead, is to love them through it. Pray earnestly for them. Pray the armor of God for them each and every morning. Tell God your desire that you long for him to step up in this area of life.

I challenge you in this, as my sisters, to sit back and let God do all the work. Here's your job: to stay faithful, to encourage, to grow in the Lord while you wait. You don't need to make the excuse that your relationship with God cannot move forward without your husband on board. You will miss out. Just purpose to daily leave this issue with God. He knows, He sees, and He has a plan. Your gentle and quiet spirit, coupled with the mightiness of God, will certainly yield some beautiful results.

When I, personally, backed off in this area, is when I saw things begin to change for the better. My heart was no longer in a constant state of bitterness. My desire was to God, and not to change my husband. And, it wasn't long until God began to draw my husband's heart closer and closer to Himself, which ultimately led us closer as a couple.

Some of our husbands deal with much deeper issues than just not being spiritual leaders or Christ-followers. I know and understand this as well. We all have sins in our lives, deceptions that we hold tight to, that keep us from drawing closer to God and one another. If your ultimate desire is to draw closer to God as both individuals and as a couple, keep the lines of communication open between you and God by remaining humble and in a constant state of repentance. God loves when we acknowledge our unquenchable need for Him. He always has our best interests in mind, and would love nothing more than to sanctify our marriages, through His grace. Let's keep focus on our own spiritual walk, and allow Christ to change and mold our marriages to mirror His image.

Us Before Them

I remember, as a brand-new mother, everything revolved around my little bundle. This tiny creature dictated when I woke up every morning, when I could eat, run errands, even when I could run to the bathroom! I recall thinking that this motherhood gig sure was never-ending and pretty thankless. How in the world was I supposed to balance a marriage and a child that demands all of the energy out of me?

I used to think it was impossible.

As a nursing mother, I would reach a point in the day where, after nursing session number nine, ten, or twelve I would wish for "a baby holding angel" to burst into my home and hold my baby for the rest of the day. In other words, I had been over-touched.

There were those rare, sweet moments when I was detached from my child and I would frolic over to the bathroom, just because. I always went, even if I didn't really need to, because chances are, baby will wake up in fifteen and then what? I may skip over to the kitchen and make myself a sweet something, maybe a nacho something, or I'd just alternate opening the fridge and the freezer at the same time because I had both hands free. Back and forth. Back and forth. Try it, it's fun.

No sooner does five minutes go by and the garage door goes up and my husband walks in, slamming the door behind him. He comes over, sees my two free hands in the kitchen, making nachos or whatever, and wants to kiss and hug and do all of those husband "I've missed you" things. Behind us, there's a screaming baby that only got a five-minute nap in because of two things: garage and slamming door noises.

With my heart sinking, I whip around, push the affection away and remind my husband to not be so idiotic when he comes home because A) we have a baby, B) I'm tired and I don't want to be touched, C) I just stopped being touched five minutes ago, and D) I now I must resume the position to be touched again. Also, E) I really wanted those nachos.

Have you ever had an encounter like mine? One where you literally grit your teeth and want to sob your eyes out at the same time? A moment where you honestly consider: "Does my husband have a brain in between those ears? Doesn't he remember the baby sleeps every single day at this time?"

Unfortunately, and this is very unfortunately, we don't

have the right to act sour towards our husbands because we're feeling "over it". Over being touched, over being caregiver, over being wife, over being a woman, period. Years later, and I still have encounters like the one I just shared. Except now, it's multiplied times five. When I have the back door opening and closing so much I should charge admission, when I have toddlers pulling my legs while I'm trying to make spaghetti, or a set of brothers arguing over who gets to ride which bike, I nearly lose it. If my husband enters when all of the chaos is boiling over, and he starts trying to turn down the heat with his suggestions, I usually snap. I think, "You've been here for thirty seconds, you have no right to say a word unless you want to pry Thing 1 and Thing 2 from my legs, take over the spaghetti, and quarantine me to my room the rest of the night".

No matter how much I justify my attitude. No matter how much I feel like a victim in those moments of chaos. I have no right to transfer that sourness to my husband.

But, I think we feel it's just natural for us, as mothers, to make sure the men in our lives know that although we may have not made a paycheck, had important meetings all day long, or delicious/paid-for business lunches, that we're tired and we need a break. After all, he is the other part of this equation here.

There are better ways to go about getting what you want. Maybe just flat out mention to him, that you see that he is tired, but once supper is over, would he mind taking over for a bit so you can get a nice soak in the bathtub? If taking baths isn't your thing, maybe you could go hide in a closet, take a super long walk to mailbox, or just drive to an empty parking lot. All of those things can be ultra-refreshing. Am I right?

The truth is, life may have changed a lot since you welcomed your firstborn, into your, once peaceful, couple-centered existence. But, it doesn't change the fact that you and your spouse should always come first. We must be willing to protect our marriages so much, that a lot of those times includes protecting our marriages from our children. Yes, they're demanding, and raising a family is hard work. Marriage, by itself, is highly demanding and exposes our deeply rooted selfishness. But, we must do the even harder work of allowing our children to witness the beauty of a marriage relationship that doesn't cater to them.

Called to Love You

I heard something, recently, that really shook me about love and marriage. There's a common belief that marriages must be completely compatible; that the other person exists to keep the other at some sort of happiness homeostasis. There is also a widely-spread view, within Christian circles, that there can only be one person out there that is meant for us.

Maybe those things are true. Maybe they aren't. But, regardless, those are the things we tend to focus on in marriage, and if your spouse doesn't live up to your expectations, well, then, you may begin to question your choice altogether. Instead of focusing on the above, focus on the fact just maybe God has called you to love that other person, your spouse. Maybe He continues to bring two opposite, unexpected, flawed humans together to expose our shortcomings, to share in our struggles, and bring us to our knees.

No, it's never easy to constantly focus on the needs of another, especially when our own selfish needs seem to cry out a bit louder for momentary fulfillment. But just like a good father continues to love his child even when they are completely unlovable, so have you been called to sacrificially love your spouse.

You have been given a task bigger than yourself. A task that is beyond your abilities. To truly love someone from the inside out is one of the greatest struggles of humanity. If you have been called to love another human, for better, for worse, in sickness and in health, for as long as you both shall live, then do it. Embrace it with all your heart and give that gift of love on the altar of Christ, moment by moment, day by day, year by year. Do it because you love Him above all else. Do it because He has inspired you to do so. He is our ultimate example in love.

> *"The LORD appeared to us in the past, saying: 'I have loved you with an everlasting love; I have drawn you with unfailing kindness.'"*
> —*Jeremiah 31:3*

Let's draw our husbands in with an unfailing kindness. Let's purpose to love them in a way that would make Christ smile and keep our homes harmonious. When we don't have the strength to do so, we know the One who can do it for us.

Embracing Eternity

"...He has also set eternity in the human heart..."
—Ecclesiastes 3:11

There's More Than Just This

Wake up. Make breakfast. Feed children. Clothe children. Get Husband out the door. Get ourselves out the door after looking for five lost shoes. Drive here. Drive there. Pick up this and that. Be this. Be that. Watch your bank account drain on pay day. Work overtime. Wish for a break. Can't afford a vacation. Laundry. Dishes. Disease. Over, and over, and over again, until we die.

I know in the thick of motherhood, I sometimes get caught on that hamster wheel of doubt. The wheel that spins the lies "There's nothing beyond this, you're doomed to repeat this cycle until you turn to dust".

Satan is rather clever, isn't he? He loves to keep us focused on ourselves and how we feel, because he knows if he keeps us there, then we have little hope and even less effectiveness.

The truth we need to be constantly reminded of, is that everything we do and say on earth, does count for something. It matters more than we can comprehend. And it will keep mattering for as long as we eternally exist.

Therefore, we need to keep our eyes on Christ always. He is the answer for an eternal life filled with prosperity. He has come that we may have abundant life! Choosing to do life under the cloud of mediocrity is not what he has for us! Christ didn't come down from Heaven to endure all He did so that you could live an average existence.

NO!

He came so that you could live, move, and breathe His Holy Name. He came so that you would know what love is, what joy can be like, and to realize that there is so much more beyond what's on this planet.

For Eternity Sake

> *"But when you give to the needy, do not let your left hand know what your right hand is doing."*
> —*Jesus, Matthew 6:3*

If there was one thing I wish you could take away from this book. More than anything else I've written; I urge you to live humbly for eternity. In other words, secretly, quietly, and without accolade, work towards your eternal reward. Here is another blog post I wrote on the subject. I hope it inspires you to do amazing things for your future.

I notice you, Christ-follower. We all did.

We saw your Facebook post. We saw your pictures of you actively serving. We saw the comments and likes that were the "atta boy" you so craved upon hitting 'send'.

And, so I wonder, truly, what has led you to believe that a virtual thumbs up or a "you are so (this or that)" comment was a great substitute for how Christ would've eventually rewarded you?

Do we read the same text? Has no one ever lovingly encouraged you, reminded you, or told you that to serve is to do so without audience?

My heart literally breaks for you when I scroll thru and witness a self-seeking, "God-honoring" post of selflessness.

You had the right intentions in serving. Oh, you certainly shared the love of our Creator to the immediate world you share with others; you may have even had the chance to develop a new friendship, invite them to your home or church, or just simply share the Gospel during the process.

You, are doing what we all should be doing. Truly. You have the dear jocy,

right idea. Christ smiled upon your obedience to Him.

"But when you give to someone in need, don't let your left hand know what your right hand is doing."

—Matthew 6:3 NLT

But the reward you sought, was as cheap as plastic. It was temporary, self-glorifying, and won't be eternally counted by the One who promised He would remember those things we did without longing for earthly recognition.

Do you really want the heart, the desire, the energy, the time you put into the giving go to waste?! Did you really, honestly think that God was proud when you traded His eternal reward for an extremely temporary version than He promised you?

Please, with love, I beg you to stop practicing this routine.

If you give money, keep quiet.

If you see a need and meet it for someone, don't mention it.

If you donate, let it end at that. Don't seek something in return.

If you love on your neighbor, don't bring up that you did so to your other neighbor.

Don't be sneaky about it either, God sees our hearts. Nothing is hidden from Him.

I wish, I hope, I pray, fervently, that you will go forth in service to others seeking ONLY His eternal praise and reward. It may feel awesome to hear how selfless you were down here, but it will never compare to being bragged on by The King of Kings someday. Never.

Secretly serve and gloriously be rewarded.

Finish Strong

I remember watching Rory Feek's daily updates on Joey during her final days. I recall watching her take those broken egg shell halves and put her little seeds so carefully in each one. I remember his photos of her getting up, as weak as she was, to make that last supper she ever made for her family. I remember their last dance, the last time she snuggled her baby Indy, and the smile on her face while she celebrated her baby's second birthday just days before she passed.

There was no greater example to me than to watch, in real time, a woman, a mother, who knew her time was extremely short, just continue to do those things that made her life worth living. The gardening, singing, teaching Indy, dancing, smiling, and inspiring, those things consumed her until her final breath.

Every day since then, I think of Joey. I think of her example to us all. I picture her in Heaven now, free from the pain and suffering she hid so graciously while on earth, just singing with Jesus. I picture her beauty, radiating without the scars of sin, just more irresistible than ever before. I picture her patiently waiting to share this life with those she left behind here on earth.

We all have a choice every single morning. That choice is based solely on our attitude towards that gift of next breath. We can choose to take those breaths for granted. We can fill them with hate, with grumblings, with frustrations and fears. We can use those breaths to remain lazy, unmotivated, and unmoved by the gift that God keeps giving to us.

Or, we can choose to breathe Him in and exhale Him out, feeling the full brevity of His plans for us. We don't need to doubt. We just need to trust. Blindly trust that He knows what you need, when you need it. All along the way, life can be as beautiful as you make it with God holding your hand.

Do You Realize How Serious This Is?

Friend, if the God-parts of this book don't make much sense to you, it may be because you haven't yet made the choice to allow God into your life. This is so serious, because you don't have forever to make this choice for yourself. In fact, none of us are guaranteed these next few moments; so all of us are living on borrowed time.

> *"How do you know what your life will be like tomorrow? Your life is like the morning fog—it's here for a little while, then it's gone."*
> —James 4:14

I want to encourage you to please consider, with all of your heart, becoming a true child of God. All you must do is admit that you are a sinner. If you take your own inventory right now, that may not be so tough to do. In fact, it shouldn't be difficult at all. How many lies have you told? Mistakes have you made? Choices that you've hidden from others?

"For all have sinned and fall short of the glory of God."
—Romans 3:23

Sweet mama, there is, fortunately, nothing you can do that could make God love you more or less. There is no measure of goodness that we can live up to in order to receive that gift of eternal life in heaven, unless we become perfect like God, Himself. Unfortunately, we've already failed. And if God is the standard, then we fall short every single time we are measured against that standard. God gives us a much easier way to achieve eternal life and that is found in just simply humbling ourselves.

Tell God that you believe that He took your place in death, placed your sin upon Himself, and died so that you could be free from sin and hell. We wouldn't choose to overlook a sacrifice like that if a stranger or a friend or relative gave their own life for us. Please, don't choose to overlook the way that Christ chose to die in your place. Don't look the other way, embrace what He did for you.

"But God demonstrates His own love toward us, in that while we were yet sinners, Christ died for us."
—Romans 5:8

After you have admitted that you are a sinner, and tell God that you truly believe what He did for you was a remarkable sacrifice, commit to Him that you need Him as the central part of your life. Just like marriage, reach out to take His hand and allow Him to gently guide you on a beautiful journey of understanding the love He has for you. He is absolutely crazy about you, and His ultimate desire is for all of us to recognize His love and choose to follow His commands for us.

"...but whoever drinks the water I give them will never thirst. Indeed, the water I give them will become in them a spring of water welling up to eternal life."
—Jesus, John 4:14

Once you commit to follow Christ, take the journey day-by-day, moment-by-moment. Christ doesn't promise us heartache-free lives filled with all of the treasures and material things we desire. Instead, as we follow Him and His purposes for us day in and day out, He is diligently rewarding us in Heaven for all of those things we do in His name.

Everything we do doesn't go unnoticed. But, only those things that we do in His love and in His will will be rewarded. Nothing else matters. I repeat: Nothing else matters.

Only what we do for Christ will last for eternity.

If you've just boldly made that decision to follow Christ for the first time, I sincerely would love to know about it and rejoice with you! Please send me a message via e-mail at dearjoeybook@gmail.com, and I will send you additional encouragement and resources to get you going on the most amazing journey you'll have the privilege to adventure on! I am so proud of the choice you've made, and can assure you that it will never be something that you will regret. An eternity in Heaven, with the God that created you, is officially in your future!

You now have all of the hope you need to tackle the rest of your life journey. You can have full confidence knowing that God will never fail you, let you down, or leave your side. You are more than life to Him! He loves you immeasurably more than we can ever hope to express!

I know that Joey is in Heaven now. I also know that we serve the same God, the same Jesus, and share the same heart for others in this life. So I know that Joey would want a book, that bears her name, to share the Gospel of the One that we should all seek to fully embrace.

To Fully Embrace

Life is beautiful. You're beautiful. God is daily offering you the grace and the resources to step into that beauty with Him. Remember how much He loves you. Remember that your hope is endless in that it doesn't reside in a finite man, but in an infinite God. Remember that when things get messy, that God is the God of the mess-makers: US! He will meet you where you are. He loves you too much to leave you to yourself.

He will constantly pursue you. He wants you to accomplish all that He has set forth for you to do in this short time here on planet earth. He desires for you to joy in your sufferings because He knows that when we keep our eyes on Him, that joy, even in the bad times, is inevitable.

My prayer for you, dear reader, is that you will embrace this gift of life, this gift of motherhood, and leave a legacy that is filled with hope, faith, and eternity. A legacy that is worth the embracing. A legacy that those who know you best would be honored to follow.

We can be thankful for the example found in Joey Feek. We can continuously remind ourselves of how she embraced life until the end. I have a feeling she left this earth with little to no regrets. But we must look beyond Joey. We must fill our minds and hearts with the Truth of God's Word in order to fully embrace this motherhood journey. Only He can give us the courage and strength to embrace it all.

epilogue

When I set out to write this book, I wasn't confident that I would actually finish it. You see, I'm a master excuse-maker. I looked at my life and thought: "This will actually never happen, you know. I have five children. I homeschool. My husband works long hours. I am tired. Goodness, am I tired. Who am I kidding? There aren't enough hours in the day to write a whole book! Plus, I have enough distractions, already."

But, I realized that God gave me this gift of writing to fulfill a purpose. That purpose is greater than anything else I could accomplish on earth. I would be a fool to not fulfill God's Will in my life in this area of giftedness.

The amount of humbling that goes into sharing my personal stories and struggles with you is sometimes hard to swallow. But, I know these stories can inspire, they can encourage, and they can, most of all, point others to Christ. This was my ultimate goal. I wanted Christ glorified. I truly hope that that goal was accomplished. Just as He was beautifully on display in Joey's life, I want to be the same sort of reflection of Him to all of you.

Joey may be the inspiration of these pages, but Christ is the purpose. I want to take the time to personally thank you for reading. I am overjoyed to be able to share this labor of love with all my readers.

If I can write an entire book while mothering, homeschooling, and caring for five children all while dealing with a massive giant of anxiety and depression, thyroid and heart issues, blogging, starting two small businesses and being a wife to my childhood sweetheart, imagine what you can do.

Satan will try to keep you from succeeding. He will do his best to distract you. He may even throw a few massive punches to your life. The only way we can rise above these attacks is by looking to the one who is Greater.

> *"You, dear children, are from God and have overcome them, because the one who is in you is greater than the one who is in the world."*
> —*I John 4:4*

I'll be cheering you on.

acknowledgements

First, I want to acknowledge my God, my Creator, my Savior, in Whom I have my greatest hope and greatest joy. He graciously gave me the gift of words, the passions in my heart, and the drive to want to change the world through the gift that is mother-hood. I am without anything without Him as the center. He is my greatest inspiration, and my complete fulfillment.

To my husband, my greatest ally and friend, I thank you after I thank our King. Without your encouragement, your drying of my tears and wiping away of my frustrations, this book would never have seen its tangible form. I am so blessed to have a husband that sees the value in my dreams and aspirations, and makes the necessary sacrifices for me to reach them. I love you beyond even what I can put into words. And that's a lot.

To my parents, for pushing me towards the dreaming. For funding the dreaming, and reminding me that I do have a voice and people want to hear that voice. I am very thankful for your support and love.

To my children, the five on earth and the one precious one I never met on this side of heaven, there would be no book without the experiences you've blessed me with. You've shown me more grace and more love than I ever hoped to experience. You keep exposing the worst and the best parts of me. I am forever grateful for what you have taught me. I love you all incredibly insane amounts.

To my siblings, I love you all and I'm so thankful for your constant love and support for this project. Specifically, to my siblings, Amber and Aric, who spent several hours of their precious time making this project look beautiful and professional. Your sacrifices to help me in this grand endeavor will never be taken for granted. Proud to be your sister.

To my friends, I love you and I'm so thankful for godly support and encouragement. For the times when I needed held, you were always there to do the holding. This book is in my hand now because of those moments.

And to Joey, the greatest motherhood inspiration I've ever had has come from you. I am beyond proud and honored to be your sister-in-Christ, to call you my hero, and to watch your faithful husband continue to keep you alive through your songs, your videos, and your precious daughter, Indiana. These pages could be filled because of the life you shared, and continue to share, with us all.

Made in the USA
Middletown, DE
08 September 2020

18389315R00086